— STEP BY STEP —
DISCIPLESHIP

—STEP BY STEP—
DISCIPLESHIP

FATHER ISHAYA SAMAILA

Kravitz & Sons

INNOVATORS IN PUBLISHING, MARKETING AND ADVERTISING

Kravitz and Sons LLC
1301 Farmville Blvd, Suite 104
Greenville, NC 27834

Published by Kravitz and Sons LLC.
ISBN:(sc)   979-8-89639-086-2
ISBN: (e)   979-8-89639-085-5
ISBN: (h)   979-8-89639-175-3

Library of Congress Control Number: 2025902807

Table of Contents

INTRODUCTION

The ministry and mission of Jesus Christ revolve around discipleship and therefore, followers are encouraged to volunteer into witnessing the gospel. The chatter for discipleship can be seen in Matthew 28:19-20 *"Go, therefore, make disciples of all nations; baptize them in the name of the Father and the Son and the Holy Spirit, and teach them to observe all the commands I gave you. And know that I am with you always; yes, to the end of time."* The Church, as the custodian of the message of Jesus Christ, explores the use of language, symbols, and signs to deepen the understanding of members and eventually their participation by putting into practice the teaching of the gospel.

This book is a product of deep meditation on the hidden treasures of human salvation hidden in the pages of the Bible; on the other hand, it attempts to apply the values of the gospel to an everyday life situation. It is one thing to listen to the gospel and another to abide by the values of the gospel. This book suggests ways disciples of Jesus Christ can radiate their thought, activities, rituals, ceremonies, and celebrations about human salvation. It is possible to follow the steps of Jesus in our spiritual journey by listening to and emulating His approach to life. As a role model, Jesus Christ had to suffer to draw our attention to goodness as a stepping stone to God through obedience.

It is often difficult to remain faithful to the life, way, and truth of God; however, despite those challenges involved Jesus Christ assures His followers that He will always be there to support, encourage, and protect His own from the devil and his agents. The contemporary world may be going through a crisis that affects life values, and cultural settings which may lead humanity into the misplacement of priorities.

CHAPTER ONE: TRANSFORMATIONAL DISCIPLESHIP

1.1. Overcome Temptations

Two monks had to travel distance across rivers for their missionary assignment. On reaching one of the rivers, they met a woman who could not cross by herself. Therefore, the older monk offered to take her on his shoulder across the river and then left her there to continue his journey to the monastery. However, the other (younger) monk thought otherwise; a monk should have no contact with women in whatsoever way. The older monk saw a situation that required assistance, which he rendered and then put at the back of his mind, but the other monk was tempted to hold him accountable for violating the vow of chastity. The scenario left an indelible impression on his mind and restlessness until he shared the story with their superiors.

The temptation account of Jesus reminds us of the encounter Adam and Eve had with the devil, who pug-nosed and misled humanity into a severed relationship between God and mankind. Adam and Eve disobeyed the instructions of God, and their ambition led humanity into suffering and death. On the other hand, Jesus, an obedient servant, embraced discipline: fasting, prayers, poverty, humility, and love to demonstrate the will of God. The devil attempted to take advantage of the human nature of Jesus Christ: hunger, weakness, exhaustion, and despair. But Jesus Christ, cognizant of His mission and ministry, chose not to do anything to jeopardize it. The devil lured Jesus into turning stone into bread to highlight human cravings for food and perishable things. Humans tend to attach themselves to consumable things like jobs, politics, and relationships conditioned for survival and sustenance.

However, Jesus Christ was conscious of the implication of going for food while leaving behind the main source of food, God. Therefore, He was resolute in saying, we live by the grace of God, not by the food we eat. The second temptation had the devil coming with a proposal on the powers of the world (politics, secular knowledge, and royalties). Whoever is in a position of leadership should be there to protect the rights of their people, serving their needs and being available. Leaders are not to extort, practice corruption, celebrate abuses, and scandalize the privileges of the citizens entrusted to them. God gives leadership opportunities to members of a community; therefore, synergy should be put in place to carry everybody along the path of God for a deeper relationship and to reach the essence of life. In the third temptation, the devil requested Jesus to worship him, there and then Jesus outrightly rebuked the devil, because only God deserved to be worshipped (as a Creator and human provider). However, mankind has difficulty in discerning what to worship; therefore, many things are idolized today: money, fashions, electronics, mobility, factories, businesses, and estates. There may be crises of interest and beliefs as a result of priorities that are mixed up. In any case, Jesus Christ remains our model and guide along our spiritual path to see temptations as ways to filter our understanding and commitment to God and His redemptive plan.

1.2. Learn from Me

A session of the gospel reminds me of our physical exercise (P.E) teacher during elementary school, who was fond of chanting, "Do as I do, don't worry." Those words meant a lot to the toddlers who confided in his leadership and guidance at that crucial time. In any case, such words further deepened the relationship and the pupils' sense of purpose. In the same way, Jesus Christ is inviting us to emulate Him, to lead others to Him to have an encounter. The slim line between being charitable and being judgmental makes it easier to switch places if care is not taken; however, we should be decisive in being relevant to a neighbor, whatever may be the case. The life and ministry of Jesus confronts the old style of doing things, especially Jewish traditions that gave leaders the upper hand while the masses may be denied legitimate rights and privileges. Jesus Christ solicits for a community that will treat members with dignity which they deserve unconditionally. Therefore, no one is made in isolation; instead, we keep in touch with reality when we assist those around us. To further reach greater heights, we must embrace the initial intention of God for humans to reflect His goodness in the world. The Christian life we live is designed to be spiritual, which may not be achieved by becoming a theologian, keeping church routines, and years of membership. Instead, it can be achieved through practicing the gospel values capable of transforming our life to an eternal one with Jesus Christ as a mediator. To achieve the maximum standard of Christian life an academic certificate is not required nor is any church field of specialization. Rather, our faith should be the basis and platform by which we can encounter God and His salvation through Jesus Christ. In the creation Act of God, the creation of mankind was at its best, but the temptation of corruption, sin, and lies might have led us to devastating consequences (death). The will of God is for humanity to live in His image and likeness which should be reflected in the way we relate with other creatures. However, the wanton destruction of an aesthetic nature painstakingly made by God is an indication that the divine assignment given to mankind is failing. Jesus Christ asks a relevant question, "Can a blind person guide a blind person?" It is pertinent for those in leadership to serve sincerely with a sense of purpose to those entrusted to their care. Therefore, God should be the center of that government to have leadership grace; instead of trusting in human knowledge, strength, and abilities. Jesus Christ as a role model made time to pray to God and further disciplined Himself in order to accomplish the mission assigned to Him. We have what it takes to secure a better life for ourselves and our neighbors; we should co-operate with God and His revelation to reach our destiny. God has great respect for the dignity of the human race; therefore, He will not take back the rights and privileges given to us.

1.3. Turn the Other Cheek

A Biblical passage encourages us to tolerate others, to be nice, generous, and patient with them. If we treat others carelessly, others may treat us anyhow too, which may make the world troublesome and in a state of instability. There was a Jewish tradition that promoted a principle of an eye for an eye and a tooth for a tooth; nevertheless, Jesus reviewed such an approach in a cordial way by conquering evil with love. His teaching laid emphasis on treating other people nicely, as a new way of living. The modern world may (proudly) exaggerate the worth of a person to enable him or her to dominate the world for selfish reasons, instead of the common good of the community. By nature, mankind is interactive, and therefore learning and practicing how to share time and space with others should be essential. We are created to be together; therefore, we need to co-operate with others in order to survive the challenges of the world. As a matter of concern, we need to learn to accept our differences; in opinions, ideas, and values to live in harmony and tranquility. Jesus Christ might have been an eyewitness to the harassment of the Roman soldiers, the bias treatment of the Jewish officials meted on their citizens. However, as a revolutionary, Jesus Christ eventually introduced a non-violent approach in interactions with others. The best way to tackle conflicting situations is to lay emphasis on how important and beneficial it is for both parties to live in peace. The dynamics of human existence cannot be harnessed through conflicts, tension, and rancor; rather it is achieved through sharing, service, and unconditional love.

Unfortunately, the world seems to be absolved by individualism and self-righteousness which places the future of humans in danger. Across human history, records of world wars, economic wars, moral breakdown, health pandemics, and abuses of religious practices are still ongoing. In a nutshell, it is self-explanatory that concepts and approaches to situations devoid of God may result in devastating consequences. The world may be degenerating to a level of putting human dignity in a very difficult position. These problems may linger for a long time until the image and likeness of God in every person whether unborn, male or female is protected. The last part of the gospel admonishes us to avoid judging others, in order to avoid judgment upon ourselves. The justice system at certain quotas of the judiciary system may tend to downplay due process by allowing criminals to go Scott-free; due to commonality and inter-relationship with those in leadership roles. On the other hand, many innocent people across the globe may be in prison for offenses they might not have committed. Both the Old and the New Testaments are drawing our attention to the 'Day of the Lord' when the ultimate judgment led by God will be. We will be rewarded according to the things we have done while our bad attitudes will be punished.

1.4. The Dynamics of Beatitudes

According to Teresa of Calcutta, "It is not how much we give but how much love we put into giving." The life we share is about give and take, as in the case of parents to their children. So also teachers, physicians, security operatives, religious leaders, manufacturers, and volunteers across all walks of life. The services people render to others cannot be quantified nor monetized as beneficiaries of those services are transformed into unfathomable joy, fulfillment, and satisfaction. "The desire of the virtuous ends in happiness, the hope of the wicked in vain... The generous soul will prosper, he who waters will be watered."[1] The world seems to be structured in such a way that those in riches and abundance may require the services of the poor around them, because they may not be able to serve themselves satisfactorily. In the spirit of complementarity and solidarity, both parties need each other for livelihood and sustenance. God in His generous tendency teaches us how to share all the things of life. To be fully alive indicates being relevant to others with the necessity of life. God initiated the creation of mankind in order to project His qualitative image and likeness; to love unconditionally, to forgive completely, and care for the needy without reservations. The responsibility of treating others kindly is innate in human existence, as it reflects God. Therefore, parents, relatives, friends, and neighbors should see it as a point of duty to reach out to those around them, who may need assistance in whatever form required. There is a quotation attributed to Pope Francis, "Kindness is firm and persevering intention to always will the good of others, even the unfriendly." What the Pope is saying in essence is that God created everything for a reason and whatever is not living according to its essence, loses its reason to exist. Life in vogue mostly across the world

---

[1] Proverbs 11:23,25

tilts towards individualism, whereby things are done according to the immediate needs of the individual, not having others in mind. This critical way of living makes us live in denial and further limits our horizon to greatness. By and large, the contemporary world is richer, knowledgeable, more creative, and more dynamic in making humans more comfortable than ever. The teachings of Jesus obviously tackle the gap created as a result of greed and selfishness perpetrated by some members who may be living in abundance while most of the community members may be lacking a decent style of life.

To live a life of sharing in common does not require one to be wealthy or one to be out of problems, but to realize that intention means so much, like the widow that gave her mite in the Bible. The lesson does not stop at rendering selfless service to others, but it rewards those who faithfully serve to the end handsomely. The life, mission, and ministry of Jesus was all about taking the problems and challenges of others upon Himself.

1.5. The Illumination of Conscience

Late former president of the World Bible Society, Pastor Dr. Kenton F. Beshore, left apocalyptic predictions in 2016 before he died. That the end of the world will be triggered in 2021, and the second coming of Jesus Christ allegedly will occur in 2028 after seven years of tribulations. The pastor strongly believed that there are sufficient signs to highlight the imminent end of the world. He noted the fall and rise of nations, wars, calamities, health challenges, shifts in priorities and the destruction of religious values.[2] In another book titled "The Warning: Testimonies and Prophesies of the Illumination of Conscience" published September 27, 2019, by Christine Watkins, she encapsulates everything. Watkins cited the personal experiences of people who almost lost their lives, but God through Jesus Christ and Hs Mother, saved them from eternal damnation. However, there is an urgent need for us to work as a team in order to overcome our physical and spiritual challenges on our journey to God. Jesus Christ was clear about His prophecies, but He reserved the exact

---

[2] 'End of the World: Deceased Pastor Left Behind Chilling Warning for 2021' ibtimesco.in Retrieved 11/15/2021.

time the incidents will unfold to God alone. The sun, the moon, and the stars have never failed to perform their functions; giving light, nourishment, and sustenance for humanity and the rest of creation. However, a closely related incident took place at Fatima in Portugal where about a hundred thousand (100,000) people witnessed the miracle of the sun which occurred October 13, 1917. "The sun, at one moment surrounded with scarlet flame, at another aureole in yellow and deep purple, seemed to be in an exceedingly swift and whirling movement, at times appearing to be loosened from the sky and to be approaching the earth, strongly radiating heat".[3] The messages of Jesus were not coercive, as He draws the attention of His audience to possibly reconcile their lives to avoid impending danger. The doctrine of 'the day of the Lord' which in Hebrew means Ha Yom Yahweh, is rooted in Judaism, Christianity, and Islam. The faithful need to be on alert and ready to face trials and challenges, and face the consequences as a result of commission and omission. Casting our minds back, we may remember that in the beginning, God created a perfect world as recorded in Genesis. However, Lucifer, the devil deceived Adam and Eve into disobeying God, thereby giving room to the first or original sin. Since then, humanity has been making efforts to right the wrong, but mankind could not succeed in doing that by itself. Therefore, Jesus Christ was the only competent savior that had to come at the appropriate time to save mankind from damnation. Although the mercy of God is greater than His justice; humans need to respond obediently to the act of kindness demonstrated by God. The catastrophes of that day will be a clear indication that God was disobeyed for too long. The day of judgment will appear like a movie, all commissions and omissions will be rolled out from the beginning of life to death. As the devil destroys life, only Jesus can save it; let us listen, He is still calling on us.

---

[3] Miracle of the Sun, Wikipedia Retrieved 11/14/2021.

CHAPTER TWO:
THE JOY OF LETTING GO

2.1. Widow's Mite

The Christian Mothers of St. Peter Claver's Parish in Otolo-Nnewi, Nigeria, charged themselves to build a hall by each donating a measure of palm kernel nuts. It was a tedious job, but they were determined to bring it to completion. Consequently, they were able to present two floors (halls) to the parish as their donation for spiritual and social purposes. Like the widow in the gospel, the women, although confronted by poverty, endeavored to make their dream a reality. The mite of the widow was a challenge to the rich, the educated, and the powerful; she gave out all she had while the rich of society offered meagre amounts. Jesus Christ observed how the Pharisees, the scribes, and the Sadducees took advantage of the masses in order to exact their authority, influence, and dominance over them. However, Jesus required leaders to live exemplary lives to encourage others to emulate them.[4] The ancient society did not have sufficient arrangements for widows (independent women); they were either under the control of their husbands or their fathers. Widows were subjected to their most senior male children as part of their inheritance. Widows had no opportunity to speak nor do anything that would draw the attention of the public to them.[5] The Biblical accounts on widows portray them as poor, defenseless, and dependent on what society offered them for survival.[6] The widow in the gospel drew the attention of Jesus by doing something extra, she stood above her lowliness and poverty in order to offer her biggest donation of two coins. The scribes had knowledge of the law and had the responsibility of interpreting them to society. However, they

---

[4] Luke 18: 1-8
[5] Dictionary of the Bible, John McKenzie, S.J P.927
[6] Acts 6:1-2

may not be there to practice what the law stipulates for all community members. In any case, the scribes and the Pharisees' donations might have required publicity for self-satisfaction. The body of Christ, the Church, has survived for over two thousand years through the generosity of members like the widow in the gospel of today. The widow did not think about her welfare nor the needs of her family members. Across the catholic world, members who may be suffering abject poverty still contribute to the progress of the Church in terms of structures, education, and the health sector. "I did this to show you that this is how we must exert ourselves to support the weak, remembering the words of the Lord Jesus, who Himself said. 'There is more happiness in giving than in receiving'".[7] The widow in question saw her contribution as important to the course of promoting human redemption (dignity) in line with a divine plan. All humans require care, love, companionship, sharing, and friendship. The culture during Jesus' time isolated widows, as they were not allowed to have a public identity or responsibility. Therefore, the treasure in the temple gave an ample opportunity to members of the community to encounter God, irrespective of their status.

2.2. Offer Everything to God

Saint Francis was born in Assisi, Italy in 1182, a catholic Friar who gave up a life of wealth to live a life of poverty. He established the Franciscan order of friars and the women's order of the Poor Ladies. He grew up leading a privileged life as the son of a wealthy cloth merchant. After receiving a vision, he was left with the stigmata (wounds) of Christ and was deeply engrossed in appreciating animals. He was canonized a Saint on July 16, 1228.[8] Like Francis, we must move into the streets to serve those facing challenges. In the history of the Catholic Church, there was an epoch that promoted monasticism across the world, which encouraged monks to embrace poverty, solitude, asceticism, and faithfulness to the will of God. They, therefore, attempted to love God with their whole mind, heart, soul, and strength. They processed the foods they ate, mended the clothes they wore, and cared for the sick members of their community.

[7] Acts 20:35
[8] www.ducksters.com, Retrieved 10/20/2021.

Such a human setting was God-centered, and He was the parameter for all activities and interactions. However, such disciplines made the Catholic Church unique and it created an identity that promoted deeper relationships with God for contemplatives and led to tremendous transformations of the Church and society. In the art of loving, there is a need to let go of valuable things in order to solidify a relationship, be it physical or spiritual. These are not in any way comparable: material possessions and human dignity. However, individualism and capitalism are rooted in our human culture, making us compete and dare into the pursuance of wealth, power, and the desire to dominate. This made St. Francis observe the suffering and poverty that occurs as a result of greed and a consumerists' culture. Jesus Christ wants us to detach ourselves from all forms of distractions arising from the use of material things, especially perishable ones. The holy men and women labeled as saints or faith heroes lived in this world with all its challenges and difficulties; yet they did not allow those things to hinder them from encountering God and His redemption. All disciples of Jesus should always model their lives after the lifestyle of their servant-leader, Jesus Christ; born in the manger, laid in a borrowed cave, a stranger in Egypt, nothing attractive about His appearance, had to borrow a donkey for a ride, borrowed a room for Passover meal, and finally laid in a borrowed grave. The kind of love we are called to practice should be selfless and unconditional service to God and His people. In the order of priorities, whatever leads us to God should be given all around attention. Just as St. Augustine observed in his Confessions: we are made by God for His sake, and our hearts are restless until they rest in Him. The consoling words of Jesus Christ are seeking first the kingdom of God and then all other things may be added unto you.[9] Furthermore, Jesus noted that His food, pleasure, joy, and fulfillment is to do the will of God.[10] We should also embrace the will to be with God no matter what and we will have no temporal nor eternal regrets.

---

[9] Matthew 6:33
[10] John 4:27-34

2.3. I Want to See

In the year 1998, barely one year after my priestly ordination, an opportunity to travel as a pilgrim to Abuja, the capital of Nigeria, to celebrate a Mass officiated by Pope John Paul II was offered to me. Celebrities in the world enjoy media popularity, which makes them household names across the strata of society. However, the man in a way draws the attention of their followers toward certain figures, either for good or for bad. Pope John Paul II, one of the most sought-after, led over one billion Catholics across the world. He appeared simple, humble, calm, and calculative in both his utterances and action. His presence is lovely to behold, and such an experience will serve as a memory for a long time. Bartimaeus faced many challenges, as he was unable to appreciate his immediate environment and could not do things for himself. The best part of his life was reduced to begging, which made him rely on the generosity of his community members. The miraculous story of Jesus of Nazareth must have reached the ears of Bartimaeus and he wished to have an encounter with the Son of David. Therefore, as soon as he realized it was Jesus that was being followed by the crowd, Bartimaeus fell by the wayside because of his visual impediment; the only available option he had was to raise his voice to receive attention. Consequently, Jesus listened and inquired to know what he wanted. We can identify with the response of the blind man (Bartimaeus): "I want to see." The ability to see can cut across all ramifications of life, as those who have eyes may lose sight of God and His good works. Therefore, in the same way, we should learn the habit of calling on Jesus like Bartimaeus to ask for the favor of perceiving His revelation through nature and the interpretation of the Holy Spirit. Blind people rely on the assistance they can get from their community members to enable them to conduct their basic activities. Due to multiple factors, God may no longer be visible as accounted in the Holy Books. Therefore, the faithful should willingly assist each other in the restoration of the vision of God's presence. As there are differences in human dynamism from one to another, we should eventually put everything at our disposal to the service of humanity and the glory of God. The harmonious existence of our physical and spiritual eyes enables us to see clearly, to further bring others to the love of God by providing food to the starving, accommodation to the homeless, available water to the thirsty, clothing to the naked, comfort for the sick, and hope for the prisoners. These corporal works of mercy make us relevant to others and make our faith active. In our spiritual journey, we often encounter deeper meaning and understanding (revelations), which should make us follow Jesus to the fullest to enjoy His salvation. The experience of Bartimaeus gives us hope, as we are encouraged to call on Jesus in whatever situations we find ourselves in, He is ready and willing to come to us to change our storyline.

2.4. Avoid Prideful Ambition

"Humility is royalty without a crown." Spencer W. Kimball

"His state was divine, yet He did not cling to His equality with God but emptied Himself to assume the condition of a slave and became as men are; and being as all men are, He was humbler yet, even accepting death, death on a cross. But God raised Him high and gave Him a name which is above all other names…"[11]

About four decades ago an uncle of mine asked to test-drive a van after Sunday Mass. Excitingly, children and teenagers jumped into the van to enjoy a 0.2-mile drive home. However, that encounter turned out to be chaotic and terrifying as the inexperienced driver went off the road and headed for a tree. My adventurous uncle endangered the lives of many children in a van so that the safety of the occupants was not guaranteed. In every given situation, humility should be the watchword. The places of honor requested by James and John highlighted the fact that the kingship of Jesus was mistaken by His disciples as a worldly affair. Therefore, the proposal of the sons of Zebedee to sit by Jesus' right and left was aimed at giving them an edge over the ten other disciples. The twelve disciples represented the twelve tribes of Israel (sons of Jacob). However, out of the blue James and John made a request that undermined the mission and vision of Jesus Christ. In other words, the request was motivated by selfishness, which provoked the anger of the

[11] Philippians 2:5-10

other disciples. Jesus earlier nick-named James and John, the sons of Bo'anerges (sons of thunder); low and behold, they took everybody by surprise with a bombshell request. Jesus quickly pointed out that the rules of engagement belong to God; whose responsibility it is to assign positions to His faithful. God rewards His followers according to their commitment and selfless service to others. As usual, Jesus Christ seized the opportunity to call on His disciples to make it a point of duty to prioritize others before their individual needs. In the Old Testament, the Israelites tried to listen to God and serve Him through responding to His messages and messengers positively. Similarly, the New Testament gospels bring salvation to the people of God through the obedience of a redeemer, Jesus Christ. The total turnover on what was in vogue was for those desiring to be leaders to preferably be servants, to render necessary services to the needy and concentrate on a common interest (salvation). Jesus Christ used 'cup' and 'baptism' metaphorically. By analogy, He assured them that they will share with Him the good things of life, its challenges, and difficulties. These speculations became real when Jesus left His disciples to bear witness to the gospel. They celebrated the nobility of bearing witness to the gospel; while on the other hand, they paid the ultimate price by dying for the sake of Jesus and His salvation.

2.5. Is not Against Us

In an article titled, "The Jihadi Who Turned to Jesus" covered by The New York Times correspondent, Patrick Kingsley, gave a testimony of a one-time jihadi, Bashir Muhammed, who fought in the Syrian civil war under the banner of Nusra, an offshoot of the Al Qaeda terrorist group. Bashir was nick-named 'irhabi' by his allies, which is the Arabic word for a 'terrorist.' He terrorized the believers of Jesus and those that practiced His gospel. However, when things turned around, other converts gathered in his house in Istanbul, Turkey to pray to God through Jesus Christ. The conversion of Bashir and others surprised many, it changed their lifestyle through reflections on the values of the gospel; they changed from being destructive to promoters of peace and forgiveness. Bashir's wife attested to the fact that he became more responsible the moment he embraced

Christianity, unlike the way he was with the Nusra terrorists.[12] Credo Catholics may detest mingling with atheists, agnostics, denominations, and people of other beliefs for fear of doctrinal confrontations. However, those who seek to have a deeper understanding may lead themselves and the faithful of Christ into what Theology is as defined by Saint Anselm, "Faith seeking understanding." Therefore, every believer in Jesus Christ should be ready in season and out of season to attend to the blind spots of our faith admirers which may, in the end lead them into genuine commitment. Those that single out themselves to degrade the gospel or the person of Jesus, somehow like Saul (Paul), may embrace the Christian faith. The inquisition from unbelievers keeps us awake and alert, to be attentive and focused on our eternal destiny. The Islamic Koran contains books on Jesus (Suratul Isa), Mary (Suratul Mariam), and Joseph (Suratul Yusuf). The problems are in the interpretations and practices of the teachings of the Holy Books. Jesus Christ taught His disciples with clear examples (parables). He showcases a child who relies on others to survive as it appears: vulnerable, docile, submissive, humble, honest, and lovely. However, the child relies on what the culture in society presents to him or her. On the other hand, Jesus Christ draws the attention of those serving to be honest and have a sense of purpose; otherwise, maltreatment may attract deadly penalties on the perpetrators. Unfortunately, there are numerous ways of child abuse: abortion, bullying, battering, starvation, sicknesses, lack of education, poverty, violence, and inattention. Human priorities may conflict with the values of the gospel, it is like a battle between light and darkness. The contagious nature of sin makes people carry guilt around, which keeps us distant from God and His plan for humanity. To overcome temptations requires self-control, discipline, and commitment to avoid using our bodies for self-destruction; instead, we should use them for the glory of God and His People. Jesus Christ exhibited absolute discipline by putting into practice whatever He taught (worthy role model).

---

[12] Patrick Kingsley, 'The Jihadi Who Turned to Jesus' Middle East, The New York Times, Retrieved 09/17/2021.

CHAPTER THREE:
IMPACTFUL RELEVANCE

3.1. The Servant of Servants

"If a man serves me, he must follow me, where I am, my servant will be there too. If anyone serves me, my father will honor him."[13]

"The best way to find yourself is to lose yourself in the service of others,"- Mahatma Gandhi.

Christology commentators are of the opinion: Jesus Christ was a silent revolutionary. He moved on from a culture that condoned slave masters to a lifestyle that had sympathy for the downtrodden and the vulnerable. Jesus solicits for a world where everybody will serve others in need, which in a way emphasizes on the fact that we need each other in order to make progress in life. The ministry of Jesus reached out to the lowly, the sick, the poor, and the marginalized. He had the needy close to Him and He attended to them based on their needs. The list of professionals that are serving humanity is endless, and their services cut across all walks of life; trained to impact the lives of others. By and large, their responsibilities contribute to coordinating and organizing the orderliness of human life. However, any feelings of irrelevance and moral temptations may lead dynamic members of society into difficulties that cannot be resolved without God. They must partner with God for a solution; otherwise, they may do something that may devastate the sanctity of life. It was the suffering of Jesus Christ that sealed human salvation. Therefore, Jesus sees Himself as a 'sacrificial lamb,' 'suffering servant' whose blood expiates human sin which serves as a sign of the new covenant. The Old Testament covenant had the tablets (Ark of the Covenant) as a symbol of the presence of God; however, in the New Testament, Jesus Christ was the full representation

---

[13] John 12:26

of God. As the disciples of Jesus, we are called to configure our lives after Him. We meet people from different walks of life that are required to be served humbly, honestly, lovely, and selflessly. We should always remember that we are the personification (alter Christus) of Jesus Christ to our generation. The Latin word minister stands for the English derivation of 'a servant,' a person who leads religious worship, government appointment, or community leadership. However, recent interpretation of the word leaves one with nuances, as those bearing the title 'minister' may not necessarily serve the people entrusted to them as expected by the members of the community. Instead, they may take advantage of those offices to acquire powers and to draw unnecessary attention to themselves. On the other hand, they relegate the people they are supposed to serve and identify with. The need for service without bias may help boost the efforts of those in positions of leadership to make positive changes and progress. Jesus Christ earned human salvation through the cross; therefore, the title of the 'Son of God' got its complete meaning in the 'suffering servant.' Jesus Christ calls on His disciples to avoid distractions in order to carry out divine assignments with a sense of purpose.

3.2. Who Am I?

The Latin saying cogito, ergo sum, 'I think, therefore I am' ascribed to Rene Descartes, a sixteenth (16th) century French philosopher, insinuates the realization of one's worth and dignity. It portrays how one is conscientious and mindful; therefore, one should live a dynamic life. It is confirmation of the fact that certain knowledge is attained or realized. However, in a world filled with uncertainties one's existence cannot be doubted. Socrates one of the fathers of Greek philosophy, said, "An unexamined life is not worth living." Although Jesus Christ knew Himself enough, He poised a question to the crowd and His disciples to hear their feelings of Him. There were so many opinions of Him; in any case, the world for over two thousand years has had divergent opinions of Him. The children of the well-to-do: politicians, kings, directors, managers, and the bourgeoisie take advantage of the positions of their parents to look down on the lowly. Sometimes they appear rude, reckless, and extravagant; the other members of society maybe wondering the reason behind it. Even after committing a crime, they may go Scott-free because of the influence of their parents.

Their activities may be drawing unnecessary attention to princes, sons or daughters of Honorables, heirs apparent. Jesus Christ humbled Himself, a divine prince that used every opportunity to serve people around Him. Through the ultimate sacrifice of Christ, the lost human dignity was restored.

Caesarea Philippi was a Roman City located in the Northern part of Jerusalem. It contained the fierce Roman soldiers, glamorous royalties, and Roman merchants. On the other hand, a Greek idol (Pan) was situated adjacent to Caesarea. It was the city of the political power of the Roman Empire in the region and a religious center of the Greeks. Jesus inquired to know their impression of Him. Therefore, it was for Him to ask, "Who do people say that I am?" His image should not be portrayed like that of Roman rulers nor appear like the Greek idol, dormant. The survey made Jesus to understand that the crowd and His disciples did not understand His personality and mission. It sounded like a bombshell to the crowd and His disciples to hear: the Son of Man will suffer, be crucified, and be raised. Peter wanted to persuade Jesus to distance Himself from such a mission; instead, in the end, Peter was rebuked by Jesus for being so myopic in his understanding and spiritual vision. To participate actively in witnessing the gospel of Jesus Christ, one needs to conquer oneself to be effective. The carrying of one's cross requires sacrifice, commitment, and absolute obedience to God. Biblical heroes abandoned their comfort zones in order to carry out difficult assignments with, and on behalf of, God. By virtue of our encounter with God, everybody is called to dedicate oneself to the service of God and others. In our individual survey, we should allow the Image of God to be reflected in our priestly, kingly, and prophetic roles as mere instruments of God.

3.3. Work for Eternity not Perishables

Political strategists present their candidates with elegance and flamboyance, to galvanize voters into voting for their candidates. Politicians dress glamorously and conduct themselves carefully; furthermore, they tend to exaggerate their manifesto in order to draw the attention of the media and for the masses to adopt their candidate. However, what they do when they enter the offices may be far from what they promised the citizens. The ministry of Jesus Christ was handy in alleviating the challenges and difficulties that confronted humanity: feeding the hungry, healing the sick, and identifying with those treated unjustly by a selective culture. Therefore, Jesus acted right away on issues without keeping His disciples nor the beneficiaries of such acts in suspense to further spur their faith. In the Old Testament, the patriarchs are called to obey, trust, and selflessly love God to the end of their earthly life. Their total submission to the will of God made it possible for them to do remarkable things from one generation to another. As they carried out the assignments given to them by God, however, they had to struggle with human nature, which severed their relationship with God periodically. In the same way, Jesus calls on His disciples to believe, obey, and live according to the divine law of human redemption. The teaching and the life of Jesus Christ is to love, to serve, to be humble, and to make sacrifices.

The use of signs and symbols in the Catholic Church made her unique and gave her a spectacular way to preserve her values and traditions. For over two thousand years, the values evolved from one generation to another, to assume deeper meaning and understanding of church membership. The use of symbols across the Catholic world leaves the membership of the Church with precious memories and appreciable feelings for a revelation of a hidden treasure of God and His actions in human salvation. As God gave the Israelites manna in the wilderness to ease their journey to the promised land, Jesus Christ, in the same way, gave us His Body and Blood to make our spiritual journey to heaven possible. The crowd asked for signs in order to believe the message of Jesus and to possibly partake in His activities. The Pharaoh of Egypt doubted the authenticity of God's involvement in the liberation of the Israelites until signs awoke him to reality; however, he was indicted by those signs and further gave room to destruction. The recent World Food Organization survey and statistics suggest that millions of people across the world may be starving due to insufficient food. More devastating and worrisome, is that billions of people in the world do not see the necessity to partake in communion (Eucharist). The salvation brought through Jesus is intended for the entire humanity in the world. But many people in the world may be doubtful of the actual presence of Jesus Christ in the Eucharist. Therefore, a sizable number of members may be dampened spiritually and thereby making their mission of completing their spiritual journey to heaven difficult or impossible.

3.4. Give Them Something to Eat

According to a 2021 global hunger survey, 690 million people across the world starve without sufficient food to live healthy life. As statistics show, many people die daily all over the world, especially children for lack of calories. The United Nations' report shows the production of foods has drastically improved; however, its distribution is still far from reaching the required goal. It is imperative for the rest of the world to concentrate on the massive production of food, not acquiring all sorts of weapons in order to give way to humanitarian projects like food security, availability of health services, welfare, and basic amenities. Food is an important element in human life. Although food production and preparation have been going through modifications from one generation to another, what food is to mankind remains the same. Food is important in every event, family gathering, celebration, and ceremony; it is displayed for nourishment, energy, and refreshment. Most dietitians are of the opinion that food can serve protective, preventive, and curative purposes, as the nutrients and vitamins in them supply the body with all that is required to live well. The Old Testament figured God fed the hungry out of His magnanimity to sustain them and to keep the plan He had going. For so many reasons the Passover meal was symbolic as it marked the Israelites' freedom, and as well it highlighted His presence as their leader. Another moment that God demonstrated care to His people was during their journey to the Promised Land as they were starving. He provided manna to sustain them on their way to the Promised Land. Basically, God in the Old Testament provided food to strengthen His people that were stranded in the middle of nowhere: "Then he (Elijah) lay down and went to sleep. But an angel touched him and said, 'Get up and eat'. He looked round, and there at his head was a scone baked on hot stones, and a jar of water. He ate and drank..."[14] The feeding of the five thousand disciples that went to listen to Jesus was an eye-opener. However, in the same way God fed His special people in the Old Testament, similarly, Jesus Christ did as well, although, He was neither a politician nor a wealthy person, but through the divine intervention of God He was able to feed His audience that were weak, malnourished, and restless. As usual, Jesus did not do the miracle of multiplying food in order to attract attention to Himself, but rather He did it out of necessity to save people from collapsing on their way back home. Worthy of note is the compassion and generosity of Jesus Christ in multiplying the food, which foreshadows the institution of the Holy Eucharist, where and when the Body and Blood of Jesus Christ are made available to feed members of the community of God's people. It is obvious that the media, politicians, religious leaders, and non-governmental agencies are unanimous in admitting the menace of spiritual, moral, and physical hunger across the world. Individually and collectively, we need to take responsibility.

3.5. Little Child, Arise!

Catholic parents and grandparents share their faith generously with their children. However, as they are sent to attend colleges or universities, they come across fellow students and professors who may not have beliefs or do not practice any faiths. Whenever such teenagers come back home with strange ideas, such reality may devastate their families. Their new scientific approach to life gives them the audacity to confront instituted facts about the sanctity of human life. They go by the nickname: millennials, as they surround themselves with electronics, music, movies, mobility, and media in general. Furthermore, they create a world of their own in social

---

[14] 1Kings 19:5-6

media with all kinds of followers that may come up with questionable characters and their secrets shared with the world. Credo Catholics are always meticulous in raising their children in the light of the faith, and in bringing them to receive the needed sacraments when due. Parents and guardians pass on their faith to their children and wards. The centurion, Jairus, demonstrated discipline and politeness in approaching Jesus, and the effect impacted his daughter positively. Although catechetical classes are gradually disappearing, it helps the Church in grooming young members to boost their faith. Catholic parents, like the Centurion, should make it a point of duty by introducing Jesus to their children, in order to be guided in life and be saved eternally. The modern means of education forms the intellectual ability of the students and trains them to be professionals. However, the human conscience is an important part of existence and requires instruction and formation by spiritual leaders. The Church is blessed with members following the steps of Jesus Christ, through volunteering into different ministries to serve the needs of our community. Intercessory prayer has a strategic place in the Catholic Church when a family member or a friend intercedes for other members or friends in need. In the case of the Centurion, he requested on behalf of his daughter to be healed. Jesus favorably listened to his request and raised her from the dead. Modern parents should have adequate time for their children in order to help them achieve mental, spiritual, and moral goals in their life. Faith is an important part of human existence as it gives the soul of the person sense of belonging and the opportunity to relate with God. The centurion knew he had a problem that he could not solve by himself, therefore he went against all odds to approach Jesus to help his dying daughter. It is human to be sick due to numerous reasons, but we need to partner with God to be healed of our illnesses. Jesus ordered the little girl to rise, grow, and be relevant in serving humanity and glorifying God. As Christians, we must look out for each other, especially those facing challenges; the way to go is through Jesus, to have Him visit the needy in our families and community.

CHAPTER FOUR:
A LEADERSHIP OF SELF-GIVING

4.1. Good Shepherd

You have failed to make weak sheep strong or to care for the sick ones or bandage the wounded ones. You have failed to bring back strays or look for the lost. On the contrary, you have ruled them cruelly and violently. For lack of a shepherd, they have scattered to become the prey of any wild animal; they have scattered far.[15]

On March 28, 2013, Pope Francis called on priests all over the world to stay close to the vulnerable, the marginalized, and to be "shepherds living with the smell of the sheep." He further laid emphasis on the need to make it habitual and deliberate.[16] Staying with the smell of the sheep, implies accompanying parishioners through their spiritual, moral, social, and political journeys. If they are happy for a good reason, their priest (s) should share in their happiness. However, when parishioners are confronted by a challenge, the priest as another Christ (Alta Christus) to the people of God, should be part of their struggle to overcome their common enemy. Year in and year out, the Church has had missionaries who volunteered (fidei donum) into witnessing the gospel in distant lands and unknown cultures. As a spiritual role model, a missionary should demonstrate impeccable character, unprecedented discipline, patience, and the ability to adapt to cultural changes. The word Pastor comes from a Latin word which means a shepherd (feeder). The pastor has the primary responsibility of leading the people entrusted to his care in all ramifications, spirituality, morality, social welfare, and holistic growth. The setting and the structure of a community may differ from one to another; therefore, it will be necessary for the shepherd to know the strategies that work better in his community. Jesus Christ, as a mentor and

---

[15] Ezekiel 34:4-5
[16] goodmissionjoyofthegospel.weebly.com, Retrieved 04/14/2021.

initiator of a new religion (Church) put His life on the line in order to leave a legacy for His disciples, which dominated His teaching and ministry on how such values should be preserved. Jesus Christ confronted some of the abusive ways of handling human dignity imbedded in Jewish culture. The ministry of Jesus did not relegate community members for any reason; rather, He re-integrated those marginalized by the culture into the community. The actions of Jesus beckon us to wash the feet of our friends, feed the hungry, clothe the naked, fast, pray, and be available to the needy. The famous Psalms 23 is edifying as well as appreciated by all walks of life, because of its inspiration that will forever remain relevant; Yahweh is my shepherd, I lack nothing… Though I pass through the gloomy valley, I fear no harm; beside me your rod and your staff are there, to comfort me… Ah, how goodness and kindness pursue me every day of my life, my home, the house of Yahweh, as long as I live. Believing in Jesus and following Him as the way, the truth and the source of life makes us sheep that are obedient to the Good Shepherd.

4.2. Love God and Neighbor in Totality

The story of *Romeo and Juliet* by Shakespeare leaves us with a commitment to each other and in a serious affection for the other. They shared feelings, understanding, suffering, joy, and challenges in order to provide the highly needed love for one another. Romeo and Juliet were admired by relatives, friends and other community members for giving life a different dimension and relevance. However, a test in their relationship cropped up when Romeo was told that Juliet died for feeling the absence of her loved one. Therefore, Romeo drank poison to do away with his life for being unable to bear the terrible loss. The death of Juliet has conspired, but on her arrival to where Romeo drank poison for her sake, she slumped and died. Love should be total, and relevance should be lost without the presence of the other important persons (God).

Jesus Christ was able to tackle the confrontation of all the oppositions which silenced them from challenging His new approach to life and its Creator. But the scholar of the law was interested in knowing which commandment is the greatest. To the listeners and the onlookers, it may appear tough and difficult to answer the question that was posed to serve as a trap or to demean the Rabbi (Master). Jesus Christ, as God the Father issued the 'Ten Commandments' set out not to contradict or degrade the values God had set out. As such, Jesus summarizes the commandments into two: love of God and neighbor. Mankind may be absolved by its immediate needs and the possibility of dominating others, which sometimes takes advantage of the vulnerable members of our community.

The concept of love, according to popular opinion, is the most used by human settings, but the most abused as well; victims of such a scam may suffer torturous relationships. What Jesus Christ is asking us to put into practice is a life of commitment that should be all-encompassing and transformative in channeling our strength, knowledge, might, heart, soul, mind, and riches in order to witness the presence of God in His image and likeness that we represent. Some spiritual Theologians categorized love into three things: 1. Agape is love that is unconditional between God and His creatures with all the necessary network to connect and communicate with people He values as precious. 2. Filia is love between a child and parents which largely comes up naturally with a bond designed by God; but this love encounters challenges like the other ones as relationships differ from one family to another. 3. Eros is love between friends and couples, which mostly bases its direction on conditions: physique, character, knowledge, talents, skills, submission, respect, dignity, and compatibility. This part of the gospel draws our attention to eternal relationship with the author of life which requires discipline, sacrifice, and commitment. Like Romeo and Juliet, we should feel irrelevant and obsolete in the absence of our other important persons, God and our immediate neighbors. The house pets we keep love totally, and to relate with God sincerely we should learn from such wholesome commitment in order to beatitude.

4.3. Nourish Your Body and Soul

During my high school boarding days, one of my classmates, Rufus, was fond of going to the kitchen to scavenge for crumps in the pantry. One fateful day, he ate more beans than his belly could take.

Therefore, he had a terrible and painful night instead of satisfying his hunger. His groaning attracted his closest neighbors, who rubbed oil on his belly to ease the horrible pain he was going through. The experience Rufus had left others wondering, is such a feeling worth it? Why should pain and discomfort be involved? Note that gluttony is a deadly sin. Jesus Christ stresses the fact that one does not live by bread alone, but by the word that proceeds from the mouth of God.[17] Jesus Christ fed His audience with spiritual food for their eternal journey before miraculously serving them bread and fish to energize them back to their destinations.

Jesus Christ withdrew to mourn the death of His cousin, John the Baptist, but the crowd needed Him desperately to reconnect and be empowered by the word of God. Jesus accepted His relevance to the needy, like a physician at a time of pandemic, saving lives should be the goal; right away, by listening and responding positively. Jesus Christ knew it was not about Him, but about those that needed His attention dearly. Having been with the crowd for a while, Jesus' disciples wanted Him to send the crowd away because it was getting late and there was not enough food to feed over 5,000 people.

The United Nations Food and Agriculture Organization estimates that about 815 million people out of the 7.6 billion people in the world, or one out of ten in the world, are suffering from chronic under nutrition as of 2016. However, most of the hungry people are in developing countries across the world. This may be due to conflicts, war, drought, and corrupt government leaders who divert federal resources for their selfish gains.[18] Today if one views television news: local, global, satellite, or listens to radio channels, reads internet journalism, or travels to some parts of the world, the reality of malnourished children and adults is so disturbing. The devastating situation calls for action as Jesus Christ did. We must stretch out our necks for others; the greatest set of people are not revered for their riches, knowledge, influence nor dominance, but for using everything at their disposal to uplift human dignity.

---

[17] Matthew 4:4

[18] Retrieved 07/21/2020.

The miracle of the multiplication of bread and fish, like the Passover feast, foreshadows the Eucharistic sacrifice, when and where Jesus Christ is not using signs and symbols but his actual body and blood to nourish and empower our troubled souls. This is pertinent as in every culture, religion, and human setting food is central and pivotal in curing, protecting and preventing agents in the body; it furthermore marks covenants, ceremonies, jubilations, and seasons. The blessed Eucharist for over two thousand years has become the life wire of the Church, it makes it unique and spectacular in reaching out to the faithful across the world irrespective of races, cultural differences, languages, classes, and values; however, the substances remain the same.

4.4. Take Your Cross and Follow

In the Tigray region of Ethiopia, East Africa a church was hewn out of a rock in the fifth century, over 1,500 years old. The founder of the Chapel in the Sky, Father Ramudda, strategically positioned the chapel in the rock to keep away enemies and to be closer to heaven. The spiritual leader of the chapel, Gebre A. Ruphuel, climbs the rock every day to pray and to serve the faithful entrusted to his care for the past 47 years. It takes two hours to trek through sharp cleaves and turns to reach the chapel; worshippers are advised not to look back as that may scare them from concentrating and keeping a balance. Gebre and his faithful climb the rock for two hours to encounter Jesus.

My seminary years, about 27 years ago, were for discerning to either pursue priesthood or fit into another profession in life. The TAN books publishers based in America got donors in the USA to sponsor sending books to aspirants and vocation nurseries across Africa (Nigeria). I was privileged to read many of their books at that time, out of which two created deep impressions on me: the first is *Purgatory: Explained by the Lives and Legends of the Saints* by Fr. F. X. Schouppe, S.J. and the second, is *The Passion of Jesus Christ* by John Piper. The providers of those books, as disciples, carried their own part of the cross by making the books available to students who needed inspiration and guidance to grow their vocation (divine call) to the priesthood.

The way of the cross (via crucis) is the safest; do not be afraid to walk along its thorny path. One does not choose his or her cross, but self- will leads one through it; your cross is prepared and appointed by divine love. Cheerfully accept the challenge. Carry your cross always without objections; do not be insolent, or step on it in vain glory, or fall under it in despair or run away from it in fear. As a true follower of Jesus take up your cross. Jesus was a cross-bearer; He leads through sorrow, you could not have a better guide, since He carried a cross. What better burden is there to carry? Endurance leads us to turn our cross into a crown.[19]

Some Christians display crosses in their churches without the dying Jesus on it, to give the devotees the impression of a risen Christ; but, for the Catholic Church influenced by St. Anselm, Bishop of Canterbury, we choose to display crucifixes with the suffering Jesus on it; to recall the highlight of Easter glory is not without Good Friday. Humanity tends to do things the easy way and if possible, pass the responsibility to others. As for the cross our model, savior, and a friend, Jesus Christ, personally took His responsibility; He committed himself to securing human salvation. Therefore, as His disciples who reflect on His teaching, His life and His values, our lives should be modeled after what will preserve such relationship and the privilege of divine encounter.

4.5. The Salt and the Light of the World

In the era of the papacy of Saint John Paul II (Carol Wojtyla) from 1978 to 2005, for almost twenty-seven years the Catholic Church witnessed a leadership that highlighted relevance at the threshold of the twenty- first century. The pope spoke 12 international languages. The pope visited one hundred and twenty-nine countries. He had a passion for the marginalized, persecuted, abused, and unjustly treated. Pope John Paul II addressed many political leaders on how to achieve world peace through justice. One of his attributes was the

---

[19] The Book of Jesus, Calvin Miller, p.353

downfall of communism in his native country, Poland. John Paul II took the gospel light and made it as tasty as the salt across the world, and not only Catholics appreciated his role as a leader but even protestants, atheists, Muslims, Hindus, Buddhists, and Jews.

In certain places, when the police stop vehicles at night for security reasons, the occupants of the vehicles are required to turn on their inner lights. This will make it easier for the security personnel to identify any dangerous weapons in the vehicles. Similarly, every baptized Catholic should let his or her inner light (the gospel) shine inviting Jesus into such life; in order to figure out how best he can help his followers with redemption through grace, love, and sacrifice. Therefore, in every given community where Catholics are present, such disciples should model their lives after the life of Jesus.

In the Biblical account, light symbolizes the presence of God: in the Creation account in Genesis, God separated light from darkness; Moses had an encounter with God in the burning bush; the Israelites on their way to the Promised Land had the presence of God in the form of flames of fire by night and clouds by day. Prophet Elijah had a contest with the worshippers of Baal who could not bring down fire to consume their sacrifice, but Elijah having instructed attendants to wet the wood and the sacrifice, he prayed for fire which instantly consumed everything that was set on the altar. In the New Testament the disciples of Jesus received the gift of the Holy Spirit which appeared on their heads in the form of flames of fire. The experience left them transformed and ready to bear witness to the gospel. At baptism, recipients and sponsors are encouraged to carry the light of the gospel to places darkened by sin.

The story of the Albanian Nun born in 1910, who adopted the name Teresa demonstrated the light of the gospel as she moved into Indian communities to pick abandoned people uncared for by the society. Mother Teresa of Calcutta had the challenges of providing those needy with care, food, accommodation, medication, clothing, and dignity. Her popular slogan was to put a smile on the faces of the needy before they die. However, within a short time Mother Teresa and her sisters of the poorest of the poor gathered about eighty-thousand homeless, malnourished, vulnerable members of the society due to human negligence. Mother Teresa died in 1997, and the world took note of the light that the needy were drawn to by doing ordinary things in an extraordinary way. We must endeavor to let our baptismal light shine and share the peace and love of Jesus Christ with the needy across the nooks and crannies of the world.

CHAPTER FIVE:
DRAWN TO THE DIGNITY OF GOD

5.1. Humility Exalts

At the launching of the British ship, Titanic, on May 31, 1911, one of the employees of the white star line claimed, "Not even God himself could sink this ship." The maiden voyage from Southampton, England took off to New York, USA on April 10, 1912. It was the largest and the most luxurious line to sail; the furnishings and the decorations were splendid. Unfortunately, the Titanic hit an iceberg at Newfoundland and sank; out of the 2,228 people on board 1,550 people died.[20] The Pharisee we encounter today presents himself as a prayerful, generous, and law-abiding man compared with the tax collector and other worshippers. The tone of the Pharisee's prayer expresses a desire to draw attention to himself and the rituals that do not necessarily radiate his spirit, in short, he lost it all like the Titanic in 1912.

God created Adam and Eve to obey and abide by His instructions; but tempted by the devil, they entertained pride and disobeyed God by eating the forbidden fruit. Pride has done more harm than humanity can imagine in history: David, Solomon, Samson, Goliath, Nebuchadnezzar, and the false prophets faced its consequences in Biblical accounts. In the New Testament, Jesus Christ sealed human salvation through obedience and humility. The clarion call is to emulate the meekness, humility, unconditional love, and selflessness of Jesus Christ in our interaction with one another and with God.

"Religious but not spiritual," or the other way round, "Spiritual but not religious," both statements may beat the imagination of the reader. The first one implies those Christians who may be following the rites and practices of their religion, but those rituals do not enrich

---

[20] Retrieved 10/10/2019.

their spirituality in any way. The "Spiritual but not religious" refers to those set of people who try to live the ideal style of life: helping the needy, resolving conflicts, sharing things in common, and ensuring justice for the less privileged. But this set of people do not belong to any organized religion, they are just good for the sake of humanity.

A young man having gotten employed, made some money, bought a car for himself and an apartment; then went to his dad to express his desire to marry the love of his life. The father looked at him intently and then sighed, "Son, to marry is noble, prestigious, and responsible. But I will only accept your intention on one condition: if you will say, 'Sorry' to me.'" The son inquired to know the reason for saying sorry but did not get an answer. Therefore, he went back home thinking deeply about the conversation if his approach was not polite enough. However, after about two trials, the third time, the son accepted to say sorry for no clear reason. As soon as he said, "I am sorry," then the father said, "Now you are ready to marry. You must learn to admit fault at times even if you think you are right or have a different opinion."

God, through the centuries of human history, has made friends that should be good to Him and to others, so also their obedience, love, and humility should be unprecedented. But God on the other hand, detests the proud, the disobedient, and the destructive people around the world. "…Wrap yourselves in humility to be servants of each other because God refuses the proud and will always favor the humble. Bow down, then, before the power of God now, and he will raise you. Up on the appointed day."[21]

5.2. Spiritual Smartness

A Carolina woman went into the local bank with a check made out to the Tension Envelope Company. In trying to cash it she claimed to be Mrs. Tension Envelope. The teller was not buying it. This was one envelope that was not going anywhere. The bank put in a call to the police, who quickly changed her name from Mrs. Envelope to Mrs. Case File.[22]

---

[21] 1Peter 5:5-7
[22] The Bathroom LOL Book p. 81

The owner of a business empire called his serviceman to account for what was entrusted to him, with a threat of being fired from his position. The master had received a series of reports on his recklessness, embezzlement, and violation of administrative ethics of the company. Therefore, the steward played the game he knew best to survive joblessness. He observed that he was not strong enough to dig, nor will he be humble enough to beg from sympathizers. As such, he chose to cheat his master, which proved his dubious ways and betrayal of trust.

The owner of the business lost valuable parts of his property within a short time. The debtors that got undeserved favor are supposed to be regular customers that should keep the business going. But their relationship with the dubious steward has categorized them with the unfaithful steward as an accomplice. The smartness of the steward is pointed out to show how serious we are in attending to worldly desires.

The steward could not be trusted with the small property; as such, he lost the confidence of bigger businesses as well. His master vested so much trust in him he was given free hands to operate, but he abused that privilege by using everything at his disposal for gratification. His mismanagement might have been happening for a while. In any case, the reckless steward did not express remorse; instead, he wanted to perfect his act of pilfering.

As pilgrims in this world, we are called to serve the Creator, God, whose image and likeness we represent in our relationships with one another and with Him. Instead, we give divided attention to his instructions by the way we live. We are being reminded no servant can serve two masters. Naturally, humans are irrelevant in the next life without God. But, if we are consumed by worldly things, the opportunity may be denied.

The essence of our worldly existence is to care for the welfare of others, thereby giving an account of the responsibilities assigned to us. If we fail in our earthly responsibilities, God may not entrust to us with heavenly responsibilities. Jesus Christ is highlighting the fact that we need to be resolute in deciding what we are up to and be prepared for the consequences. In the Old Testament, God is portrayed as always faithful, while the people were inconsistent in relating with Him and their fellow humans. Thus, they endangered the trust God placed in them.

5.3. Voluntary Disciples

The liturgical life of the Church is ideally suited to marking the decision to "drop the net" and follow Jesus for both individuals and the larger community. This can take many forms, such as the commemoration of one's baptismal day or first confession. Many evangelization processes and retreats have built-in "markers." Nothing fosters a widespread culture of discipleship like seeing new disciples from all backgrounds emerge in the parish.[23]

The culture we live in connotes individualism, which dwells so much on the welfare of I, me, and myself alone. But the golden standard in the Church is taking care of a neighbor before oneself. The first disciples of Jesus worked hard to preserve the status quo; the whole group of believers was united, heart and soul; no one claimed for his use anything that he had, as everything they owned was held in common.[24]

"'See now, this has touched your lips. Your sin is taken away. Your iniquity is purged.' Then I heard the voice of the Lord saying: 'church would appear disfigured.'"[25]

Bonhoeffer Dietrich opines, "Christianity without discipleship is always Christianity without Christ." It suffices to say if one receives the faith at any time, it is through the kindness of voluntary messengers of the gospel. Therefore, the beneficiary of a faith encounter should take the task of sharing the good news with others, as well.

Saint Paul admonishes an ideal disciple should be armed with the inspired Word of God, good enough for teaching, correction, reproof, and training in righteousness in order to have a complete

---

[23] Sherry A. Weddell, Forming Intentional Discipleship p.182
[24] Acts of the Apostles 4:32
[25] Martin C. Albl, The Church Christ in the World Today p.212

man or woman of God equipped and ready to serve.[26] The message does not depend on the disposition of the disciple. Instead, the disciple should be seen as an instrument used by God to bring the message of salvation.

The triumphant Church is a multitude of Saints that lived in this world despite the chaos and the challenges in it; but submitted to the will of God to achieve holiness in order to gain entrance into heaven. It should be the utmost desire of every disciple to be Saintly (holy) to merit heaven. Such heroes exhibited discipline and practiced their virtues in order to configure the presence of God in their communities. A disciple or a Christian is a pilgrim who should follow the steps of the saints to model his or her life according to the standard set by God.

5.4. Humility, a Mother to Other Virtues

Always consider the other person to be better than yourself so that nobody thinks of his interests first but everybody thinks of other people's interests instead… Jesus' state was divine, yet He did not cling to His equality with God but emptied Himself to assume the condition of a slave and became as men are; and being as all men are, He was humbler yet, even to accepting death, death on a cross.[27]

According to St. Alphonsus Liguori in his book Moral Theology Volume 1, Books 1-3 (1-3) p.461; it says of pride as being a "disordered appetite for one's own excellence; it is a mortal sin by its genus if it is consummated and carried out, i.e., if someone so desired to excel that he refused to be subject to God, superiors, and their laws. Instead, such a person makes himself or herself a god with laid emphasis on abilities, knowledge, power and material wealth."

The devil met a monk, Abba Macarius, heading to his monastery cell; with the intention of striking him, but he could not. Out of frustration, the devil started ranting, "As you fast, I can starve myself

---

[26] 2 Timothy 3:16-17

[27] Philippians 2:3-8

as well; as you keep vigil, I can also deny myself sleep; but there is one thing you have which I do not have." Macarius asked, "What is it?" The devil answered, "Your humility is unprecedented, which makes you impenetrable."[28] This reiterates the words of St. Augustine, "Humble yourself and God will descend to unite Himself with you; but if you are proud, He will depart from you."[29]

The Pharisee stood there and said this prayer to himself, "I thank you, God, that I am not grasping, unjust, or adulterous like the rest of mankind, and particularly that I am not like this tax collector here. I fast twice a week; I pay tithe on all I get." The tax collector stood some distance away, not daring even to raise his eyes to heaven; but he beat his breast and said, "God be merciful to me, a sinner." This man, I tell you, went home again at right with God; the other did not. For everyone who exalts himself will be humbled, but the man who humbles himself will be exalted.[30]

The author of the book of Sirach Chapter 3 makes a relevant point about humility; if one conducts his or her affairs with humility, the rest of the world and God will celebrate such a person. To the extent, a humble person is preferred to a generous person. Therefore, the virtue of humility requires simplicity, contentment, patience, meekness, and docility. In the second reading, letter to the Hebrews, God in the Old Testament is portrayed as a scary creator who spoke with a thunderous voice to His people. But, in the New Testament Jesus Christ, through his words, action, and blood spoke more eloquently.

The gospel of today teaches us a lesson on taking seats that are low in order to responsibly position oneself where he or she belongs. In Nigeria, my original country, politicians have a dramatic way of elevating their status. They appear polite, courteous, and responsible when campaigning. But the moment they assume office, they metamorphose into tyrants, miscreants, and nuisance as they drive around with a long entourage, heavy security, and sometimes spread

---

[28] Quotes of the Fathers, Retrieved 08/21/2019.

[29] Alphonsus Liguori, The Twelve Steps to Holiness and Salvation, P.124

[30] Luke 18:9-14

money for the masses to be trampled upon. The unfortunate thing is that once they are out of the office some of them turn out to be beggars. The exalted are thereby humbled.

5.5. Listening to the Poor

Deacon Lawrence was born in 225 AD; one of the seven chosen deacons assigned to serve in Rome. He was appointed to care for the treasury and riches of the Church and to distribute alms among the poor. In the year 258 AD, emperor Valerian the prefect of Rome during persecution, asked Deacon Lawrence to turn over the riches of the Church to his authority. Deacon Lawrence requested three days to assemble the wealth of the Church. Thereafter, he started the distribution of the property of the Church to the poor to prevent the emperor from seizing them. The third day, a delegation from the emperor came to supervise Lawrence's declaration of Church treasures: he presented the poor, the crippled, the blind and the suffering, and said these were the treasures of the Church. "The Church is truly rich, far richer than your emperor." At the end, Deacon Lawrence was killed in a horrible way. He was grilled to die slowly; and he noted, "I am well done on this side. Turn me over!"[31]

Jesus admired the young rich man who observed the precepts of the law and practiced his religious rituals regularly. However, he was deeply religious, but not spiritual as the teachings of his religion could not assist him to detach himself from his wealth in order to serve God through the needy. The Biblical models approached life differently; Abraham left behind his land and relatives to obey God. Similarly, Moses left the animals of his father-in-law in order to lead the people of God (Israelites) to their promised land. The ministry of Jesus Christ had the poor, the sick, and the marginalized as the core of his gospel. The reason for our invitation by Jesus Christ is to voluntarily embrace discipleship by being helpful to those in need of necessities. The young man attached himself to his wealth, so much so that it obstructed his view of God and what he could possibly do to alleviate the suffering of others. The greatest set of

---

[31] St. Lawrence and the "Treasure of the Church" https//www.ccmke.org retrieved 09/30/2021.

people in this world are those who spent their lives serving others to their maximum capacity. Mother Teresa of Calcutta said, "This is the meaning of true love, to give until it hurts." But on the other hand, some of the wealthy may rather concern themselves with what to add to their account; to make themselves proud and dominant over others. God appreciates and rewards every effort we make in reaching out to others and by making them feel better. The world is made in such a way that sharing is inculcated into our daily interactions: parents to their children, friends complement each other, coworkers help each other to attain goals, teachers impart knowledge, military, police and other security agencies volunteer into protecting their citizens. Jesus Christ observed how children appear simple, obedient, docile, humble, forgiving, respectful, and submissive to authorities. Likewise, the disciples of Jesus Christ should emulate the virtues of children in order to attract grace and salvation.

CHAPTER SIX:
COMPLETE SELF GIVING

6.1. Love One Another

"War is what happens when language fails." "Only the dead have seen the end of the war." "The true soldier fights not because he hates what is in front of him, but because he loves what is behind him."[32]

The world seems to be filled with hate, animosity, and vindictiveness which may be glaring in relationships and interactions. In the new teaching of Jesus Christ, love is its core which requires us to serve and care for the needs of others in our community. However, mankind to some extent, is entangled in individualism which devastates a culture of togetherness, sharing, and concern for the welfare of others. As observed among babies, they are open to the generous gift of love through care (touch); however, whenever they do not get it for a moment, they cry for attention. There is an innate natural desire for humans to love their kind; while, on the other hand, an extra energy is required to hate another person. Jesus is clamoring for humans to live according to its nature by making others feel good.

God created the universe out of love. Therefore, God loved us first and He requires love from us through obedience and faithfulness. However, from one generation to another, humanity dents our relationship with God and with fellow humans out of self-centeredness and disobedience. The need to impact the lives of others is needed more than ever before, as divisions are on the increase due to numerous factors. Having the commandments, the sacraments, the corporal works of mercy, and the virtues are all making a clarion call for honest commitment and selfless service, wherever disciples have a responsibility. The scriptures and the traditions of the Church,

---

[32] quotabulary.com

as reflected in the dynamic activities of the Church, are never in conflict with each other in whatsoever way. Rather, both scriptures and traditions are always unanimous in encouraging disciples to love and serve God and His people unconditionally.

The world encountered wars, conflicts, and other manmade disasters that terminated millions of lives and left many more devastated. Other creatures in the world had never engaged themselves in meaningless killings to prove their pride or dominance in a world owned by God. The presence of Jesus is for human redemption and reconciliation in order to reach a complete image and likeness of God through selfless service. The contents of the Old and New Testaments are disclosures of divine love through the patriarchs, the prophets, the priests, the kings, and the disciples. Some Biblical commentators think that the scripture is a narrative of the love story of God for His people. Saint Paul sees divine love thus: Love is always patient and kind; it is never jealous; love is never boastful or conceited; it is never rude or selfish; it does not take offense, and it is not resentful. Love takes no pleasure in other people's sins but delights in the truth; it is always ready to excuse, to trust, to hope, and endure whatever comes.[33]

6.2. Attentive Disciples

The ministry of Jesus started like other ministries, but his simplicity and servant-leadership strategy differentiated him from other religious leaders. Throughout his ministry, he practiced physical, moral, and spiritual disciplines in order to lead by example. Jesus chose messianic secrecy to keep away unnecessary attention from himself. He comes to bear witness to the greatness of God, whose goodness and mercy made redemption possible. The miracles in the gospel during Jesus's ministry complemented the restoration of human dignity. The central message of Jesus is serving others through unconditional love.

The teachings of Jesus leave his disciples with practical ways to keep in touch with God and others. The corporal works of mercy (feeding

---

[33] 1Corinthians13:4-7

the hungry, clothing the naked, visiting the sick, giving water to the thirsty, visiting those in prison, accommodating the homeless, and burying the dead); serve as a standard for Christians to better the lives of others in need and to further deepen their relationship with God. The Jewish authorities saw Jesus as a threat to an abusive culture that the rights of the low classed citizens of the community were denied. The tension between leaders and the masses was obvious; however, Jesus insisted on unconditional love, selfless service, and forgiveness from all strata of life in whatever situation.

As the disciples of Jesus began witnessing the gospel, they had to be resolute either to succumb to the pressures of the authorities or to go by the direction of the way and the truth, Jesus Christ. Therefore, they endured beating, imprisonment, starvation, and hostility from other cultural settings against Christian discipleship. To participate in the gospel will require a disciple to emulate the deeds of our Lord and Master, Jesus Christ, who faced humiliation and suffering and at the end had to die. Suffering makes us humble and gives us the opportunity to reflect over what we lack and the best way we can obtain them through God. Job in the Old Testament suffered the loss of his family members, riches, health, and friends as proof to his obedience and commitment to God.

The followers of Jesus should always listen to His voice amongst other voices, multiplication of religions, internet, satellite, electronics, and mobility. Disciples of Jesus should be resolute in keeping in touch with Him and His way of life. The distractions are on the rise and may eventually affect our values and activities. In the Old Testament, God protected the Israelites from the land of slavery (Egypt) along their journey to the promised land (Israel). However, the journey expected to take forty days ended up taking forty years to arrive at their destination. It was made possible out of the goodness and generosity of God. In the same way, Jesus Christ is leading His followers out of slavery to sin into spiritual freedom or eternal salvation. The Faithful of Jesus Christ should keep listening to the voice of a savior, who would rather inconvenience Himself than let down His followers. Our bucket list may be long, but a future without Jesus Christ may be doomed.

6.3. Divine Mercy

Mother Teresa and her Sisters of Charity (5,167 by 2020) serve the needy that may be left joyful and with feeling unworthiness, to be served by the angelic hands of the sisters. They truly reflect the image and likeness of God in the world; and therefore, anybody who serves them is serving God in His full nature. The Charity Missionary sisters go into human settlements to pick up people abandoned by society from the garbage, the gutters, dilapidated buildings, the streets, and market squares. The mercy of God is what humanity enjoys without merits to justify such kind and generous actions of God.

If you never overlooked our sins, Yahweh, Lord, could anyone survive? But you do forgive us: and for that we revere you.[34] The world through generations is filled with bizarre cultures that may be seen by modernists as civilization or progression. The abortion of unborn babies is ongoing to protect the ego of the indisposed supposed to be a mother. On the other hand, at old age society considers senior citizens as irrelevant and burdensome to the economy and a waste of space. Therefore, the idea of euthanasia or mercy killing is inculcated in them to choose to die, which undermines the sacredness of life that belongs to God alone. Other humans are also destroyed for selfish reasons: wars and conflicts annihilate people of all ages and those that survive are left with a devastation that will take generations to overcome. May the mercy of God absolve us in our life journey, for we have fallen short of His goodness and glory.

God endowed humanity with the ability to serve one another, but every given opportunity seems to be exploitative and may divert resources into personal belongings; instead of working for the common good of society. The gap between the rich and the poor, the leaders and the fed is glaring as the wealth and resources of the world are in the hands of few, while most people in the world live

---

[34] Psalm 130: 3-4

in abject poverty. As God is generous and caring in giving us the necessities of life, we need to extend hands of kindness to impact the lives of others around us.

Mercy is an act of kindness to a person that does not deserve it, but out of the magnanimity of God, He leaves His comfort zone in order to restore our lost dignity. As far as God is concerned, there should be no judgment by His standard. Humanity may not deserve anything but condemnation. However, God tempered justice with mercy; and therefore, He is still in control as things go on according to His direction and will. We were first loved by God,[35] even if the world will hate and maltreat us; however, we should rather preserve His image and likeness in this world than compromise. The love and mercy of God has been there through generations proving His providence and unconditional generosity irrespective of our disposition and commitment to His invitation and service to His people in the world.

6.4. Bring Others to God

The art of fishing with the nets and the boats were all in good shape; however, the grace of God was nowhere to be found. Jesus noticed the uneasiness: frustration, anxiety, exhaustion, and the overwhelming pressure of their families. Therefore, Jesus taught them how to face their fears, worries, and troubles; and a better way to overcome their challenges. The fishermen relied on their skills and the tools of work they had, thereby isolating the role of God in their lives. It is equally important for us as well, to always invite God before embarking into our daily activities, to be assisted by the God of generosity and providence. Peter, Andrew, James, and John probably considered the invitation of Jesus Christ as an opportunity to upgrade their horizon, as they might have realized that fishing was becoming more difficult while the burdens of their families lingered. In any case, they dared to leave their comfort zone and known profession to go with a man that surprised their imagination (miracle of greatest fish catch). Their recruitment took place instantly and went ahead to submit themselves for tutoring, on how to draw others into a new

---

[35] John 3:16

religion through friendship and service. The new recruits relied on the guidance and teachings of Jesus Christ, on how to be relevant in His ministry and mission. The basis of Christianity by and large is discipleship, which occurs as a result of invitation we receive from Jesus Himself in one way or another. In the recruitment of His apostles, Jesus did not consider human standards which may take into cognizance their fields of specialization, family background, and their ability to attract members of the community, even those in authority. Instead, Jesus proved the fact that every human person is capable of being dynamic, creative, and wonderful in rendering great services to humanity. Therefore, in giving an assignment, God looks at the inner ability of the person not his or her appearance, as in the choice of King David.[36] The fishermen got a better style of life for accepting to bear witness to the gospel, from fishing in a filthy atmosphere into meeting the needy people around them. In that instance, the fishermen dropped their nets, and they gave up everything to serve Jesus and His ministry. Peter, Andrew, James, and John had to literarily leave their nets (profession or means of livelihood), family members, and friends to be with a man (Jesus Christ) whom they did not know much about. However, the openness and friendship of Jesus attracted them to see in him a capable leader, able to lead them into a meaningful life. These four chosen apostles became the closest to Him and His ministry. Jesus had them by His side at important moments of His ministry. The lesson we can learn was the way they responded to Jesus' invitation, "They left everything and followed him." Similarly, we need to respond to the invitation of Jesus Christ, to serve as witnesses to the gospel. One may wonder why Jesus Christ did not invite scribes (lawyers), wealthy Pharisees, religious priests, or Roman soldiers. The gospel is needed more than ever before, as more conversions and membership are taking place at an alarming rate, every member should consider where and how to volunteer into witnessing.

---

[36] 1 Samuel 16

6.5. Be a Herald

Political presidents, majestic royalties, and other supreme leaders move around with formidable security agents to ensure their safety and easy facilitation of their functions. In the case of Jesus, he chose John the Baptist to nicely inform his listeners about his coming as a messiah; and therefore, their hearts, minds, and daily styles of living should be reviewed to correspond to His mode of operation. Contemporary bodyguards always use whatever they have at their disposal to scare others around them. Sometimes, situations may be out of their control. On the other hand, John the Baptist isolated himself from a busy community into the desert, he went to teach those that appreciated his message in order to find relevance and meaning of life. The baptism of repentance preached and carried out by John the Baptist served as a preamble to the coming of savior, Jesus Christ. Although John the Baptist did not have complete power to reconcile us with God, but attempted to introduce us to the savior of the world (Jesus Christ) and to God our creator. Therefore, John the Baptist is like a signpost, it points to something greater than it is; Jesus Christ remains the subject and the object. John was conscious of the fact that his cousin, Jesus Christ, who was six months younger than him, was by far greater than him. John shared the uniqueness of Jesus with his audience throughout his life, who excitingly expected the Son of God, who appeared greater than dynamic and disciplined John the Baptist who was consumed by holiness and service. Preparing the way is all encompassing: one's house, moral conduct, spiritual commitment, and inter-relationships should correspond to the teachings of Jesus Christ. This discipline will require leaving one's comfort zones and change of a culture that is demeaning to human dignity to a responsible option instituted in Christ. The challenges prior to the inception of John the Baptist were despair and lackadaisical attitudes toward God's messages through priests, kings, and prophets. For John the Baptist introduced a different dimension to life; he appeared in a spectacular way and invited his audience to await a unique man in all His ramifications. However, as the coming of Jesus attracted the prophets, priests, and kings, as well as their audience, who were eager to welcome him. But in His simplicity, Jesus, chose to identify with the ordinary members of the community. Jesus Christ left this physical world for over two-thousand-years (2,000) now; that notwithstanding, it is still needed to prepare our hearts, minds, and homes for His second coming. There is a clarion call all over the world for disciples to volunteer into bearing witness to the deeds of Jesus and why He went back to heaven to prepare a place for us and to make possible His second coming. The final mission of Jesus is to provide mercy and justice to humanity. In addition, God desires people that are obedient, faithful, and committed to the original plan of uniting with God forever.

6.6. Mustard Seed

The Chinese bamboo tree must be planted, watered, and fertilized and yet it takes five (5) years to break the ground. As soon as it breaks the ground, after five years it will grow up to ninety (90) feet within five (5) weeks. It requires patience, dedication, care, availability, and unalloyed commitment to achieve the required result. It takes the bamboo half a decade to surface, but as soon as it comes out, then humans, animals, and birds can benefit from it in all ways. The idea of planting mustard seeds or bamboo trees may sound odd to a pessimist, as anxiety may take advantage of such a person to the point of losing interest. Endurance and doggedness are required in order to achieve a dynamic result. For a farmer, the process of planting is ongoing by seasons, however, he must verify the potency of the seedlings to ensure the possibility of having seedlings that will germinate. Similarly, the soil should be prepared and fertilized to boost the growth of the plants. The farmer may select good seeds, cultivate the farm, and apply fertilizers but the rainfall, the growth of the plants, and how much will be harvested will simply be by the grace of God. It has been established that all living creatures depend on plants for food, shelter, protection, and sustenance. Furthermore, scientists are of the opinion that trees during photosynthesis boost the supply of human air while trees need the carbon dioxide extracted from humans and other animals; we are interdependent. The process of planting a seed and how it grows is a two-sided coin: the first side is carried out by humans; planting and cultivation. But its other side, the growth and fruitfulness of the plant, completely depend on the providence of God. Across the world there are varieties of plants from one region to another. Beautiful sets of flowers are all over the world; they gladden the heart and decorate our human environment. In a nutshell, the mystery of the presence of God is imbedded in His aesthetic handiwork in the creation chain. Jesus Christ figures the kingdom of God as reflected in the gospel, as a seed (mustard) that started in a humble beginning, but endurance and commitment will let it grow into all ramifications of life. To harness the gospel is as difficult as planting a seed; as patience, dedication, humility, and selflessness are required to enable growth. The parable is an expression of the prophetic role of Jesus Christ, on how the kingdom will spread to the four corners of the earth and all nationalities will partake of it. The seed of the gospel commissions disciples into serving others and bearing witness. The corporal works of mercy of giving drink to the thirsty, feeding the hungry, visiting the sick, visiting those in prison, burying the dead, clothing the naked, and sheltering the homeless can enable us to provide succor to the needy. Jesus as our model and mentor taught us how we can serve as another Christ to all generations.

CHAPTER SEVEN:
RECONCILIATORY SACRIFICE

7.1. Redemptive Mercy

The coming of Jesus Christ as foretold by the prophets, the priests, and the kings in the Old Testament, portray Him as a suffering servant who later sealed the redemption of humanity through His passion and resurrection. The core of the ministry of Jesus Christ was to tackle the challenges of human life in this world and the next. The mercy of God, through Jesus Christ, is the unmerited grace humanity is opportune to have. However, for humanity to enjoy the fullness of the salvation received through Jesus Christ; we are expected to volunteer into discipleship in order to partake in bearing witness to the gospel. The cross of Jesus Christ is a source of inspiration since the third century, when the mother of Constantine, the Roman Emperor, Saint Helena, discovered the original cross on a pilgrimage to Jerusalem. The cross of Christ for centuries has served as a symbol of victory, love, and hope. Although, as sinners, we do not merit the ultimate sacrifice by Jesus Christ yet, He is inviting us to participate fully in His kingdom. Come to me, all you who labor and are overburdened, and I will give you rest. Shoulder my yoke and learn from me, for I am gentle and humble in heart, and you will find rest for your souls. Yes, my yoke is easy and my burden light.[37] A story of a legendary rider who crossed the frozen Lake of Constance by night without noticing it. And on the other side, when he was told about the risk of crossing the snow belt, it scared and horrified him. Similarly, as spiritual pilgrims we go through challenges, difficulties, and trials. But the pivotal role of Jesus will not let us see the dangers we go through; until finally our salvation is secured through t he victory of the cross. Jesus Christ, conscious of the consequences of taking human form, notwithstanding, successfully accomplished

---

[37] Matthew 11:28-30

49

the economy of human salvation. In our responsibility, we must cooperate with God through Jesus Christ in order to be made worthy citizens of heaven. Traditions and Scriptures of the Church contain the deposit of faith that gives the faithful the opportunity to gain their indulgences. Therefore, Easter glory brings to us grace, a supernatural gift that we acquire through the sacraments and other devotions of the Church. The divine mercy devotion was initiated by Jesus Christ, just the same way God initiated the creation of humanity. In a vision, Sister Faustina Kowalska, a Polish Nun, was guided by Jesus Christ on how to recite the prayers. Although, at the inception of Divine Mercy devotions, many challenges confronted it, eventually the rest of the world embraced it as one of the best ways to reflect the passion of Christ. There is testimony of a family devoted to Divine Mercy devotions who shared their encounter with the rest of the world. One unfortunate night, armed robbers succeeded in entering their house, but the strategic image of Divine Mercy illumined the atmosphere which scared away the armed robbers.

7.2. The Cost of Discipleship

An evangelizer was sent to a community to bear witness to the good news of our Lord, Jesus Christ. Upon arrival, the people welcomed the pastor and went ahead to introduce him to their community chief, whose son was in a comatose state due to an ailment. The chief listened to the missionary attentively and then gave permission for any missionary activities in his jurisdiction. Therefore, the evangelist was led to the room where the sick child lay to begin his prayer session with the hope of healing the young man. After so many hours of prayers, the child started moving and eventually got completely healed. There was jubilation in the entire community and there-after the chief, his household and the community members embraced the new Christian faith. The sacraments we receive in the Catholic Church empower us to understand and share all their goodness as revealed through the gospel. In other words, every recipient of the Catholic sacraments should be a voluntary disciple who should readily serve God and His people. But, for a disciple to carry his/her divine assignment, there is a need for a one-on-one encounter with Jesus, who serves as a model and the core of human salvation. The disciple should be acquainted with the teachings and actions of Jesus in order to represent Him wherever and however possible; to bear witness to the gospel of Jesus is all-encompassing. Therefore, in our narratives, there should be harmony between the historical Jesus and the Biblical Jesus on the Cross, and imaged in our neighbors. The call of Peter, Andrew, James, and John was dramatic, they instantly had to leave their means of livelihood and their families to delve into a mission that was at that time vague to them. No one voluntarily sheds his or her job, home, and whole way of life accidentally or unconsciously. Simon Peter's "drop the net" decision is what we mean by "intentional." From the moment he dropped his nets to follow Jesus, he was a disciple.[38] By statistics and survey the number of unemployed in the streets of Jesus's time could be in huge numbers; Jesus carefully selected his disciples not measured by any human standards but attracted by their spiritual values. This explains why Jesus did not pick scholars (scribes) of the law, wealthy Pharisees, nor priests. Rather, Jesus went among the koinonia (commoners) to pick his companions to have the poor close to his heart who look forward to a dynamic gospel that radiates justice and peace in the world. Our generation faces the challenges of great division between light from darkness, right from wrong, good from bad, and a savior (Jesus Christ) from a destructive devil. The presence of Jesus in the celebration of sacraments, tabernacles, adoration chapels, on the Cross, the poor, and the persecuted is the game changer in making human life meaningful with a destiny.

7.3. Come and See

A Monk goes through villages on his way to the mountain for prayers and meditations. Gradually, the community members were drawn to what took the attention of the Monk. Therefore, enthusiasts followed him to where he chose to go in admiration of his commitment and the direction of his energy. Eventually, people joined the movement that drew the attention of the whole community. The Monk in his own way brought meaning into the lives of the communities around

---

[38] Forming Intentional Disciples, Sherry A. Weddell P.65

him. Just like the disciples of John the Baptist who encountered Jesus. As of this time the vision and mission of Jesus were not yet assimilated by the surrounding communities. Jesus embraced His Father's business (raising the dead, healing the sick, feeding the hungry, freeing the captives, giving hope to those that were hopeless, and reconciling differences through forgiveness).

Jesus Christ taught His audience, with a good strategy of making friends, who voluntarily became His disciples. As a leader of a new religious movement, Jesus was down-to-earth and open to all followers in order to carry everybody along. To Jesus, His mission and ministry were more important to Him than living in a flashy mansion, thus in his words: "Foxes have holes and the birds of the air have nests, but the son of man has nowhere to lay his head."[39] The generation of Jesus Christ might have witnessed golden kingdoms of the royalties, the mansions of the politicians, religious leaders, and the rich. The world seems to base its standard on what a person acquires in order to be respected in society. Therefore, the latest disciples of Jesus saw a new perspective of life that centralizes everything on the dignity of human life.

A disciple of Jesus does not need to have mansions, political power, or any form of material dominance but a soul that is willing to use hands, legs, eyes, energy, and resources to serve the needy in the neighborhood. The transparency of Jesus galvanized His disciples to the point of sticking to their newly discovered master and further invited relatives to encounter a deeper spiritual life. As Andrew and John ascertained the authenticity of their teacher, they went into evangelization that brought Simon's son of Jonah to Jesus. Jesus saw the qualities of leadership in Simon; and therefore, he named him Peter which means "rock" on which the assembly of His (Jesus') followers will stand. Jesus Christ embraced poverty and simplicity to identify with the homeless, the poor, the sick, and the lonely. Every purposeful leader should lead by example; by implication, their style of life should correspond with that of the commoners (koinonia) in society. In any case, if the members of the society are languishing

---

[39] Luke 9:58

in the streets for lack of accommodation and basic care, while the leaders of the society are comfortable in their mansions, they are busy digging ditches instead of bridges. The invitation to come and see where Jesus Christ is, is still on going, to avail everybody the opportunity to encounter Jesus Christ to understand His mission and ministry.

7.4. Treasure Hunt

Forrest Fenn, a wealthy New Mexico resident in the USA, an art dealer offered only a short poem to serve as a hint to those interested in hunting the hidden treasure: "Begin it where warm waters halt/ and take in the canyon down/not far, but too far to walk/put in below the home of Brown." The search for the treasure weighing about ten pounds of gold medals, artifacts, gems, jewelries, and valuables worth millions of dollars was the talk of the town for a decade. The game of searching for the treasure attracted over 350,000 people across all walks of life; some went as far as resigning their regular job appointments to dedicate their full time and energy into searching for the hidden treasure. The search went on for over ten years, before it was finally discovered by a man who chose to remain anonymous; unfortunately, five people died in the process of searching for the revered box at different times. Forrest presumed it will bring people out of their couches and away from their TV screens into an adventurous journey, probably into a fortune for life. The kingdom of God is a hidden treasure, which so many people have not seen its worth and dynamic transformation.

In the Church, there is a spiritual treasury made up of the superabundant merits of Our Lord, the Blessed Mother, and the saints. The merits of the passion and death of Our Lord are infinite, for He is God. All these He left for His Church. When the Church grants an indulgence, it does not really cancel any expiation due to God. It only supplies for our deficiencies by drawing on the spiritual treasury of the Church, exercising the power of the keys given to Peter by Christ.[40]

---

[40] My Catholic Faith, Louis La Ravoire Morrow P.335

God, infinitely perfect and blessed in Himself, in a plan of sheer goodness, freely created man to make him share in His own blessed life. For this reason, at every time and in every place, God draws close to man. He calls man to seek him, to know him, to love him with all His strength. He calls together all men, scattered and divided by sin, into the unity of His family, the Church. To accomplish this, when the fullness of time had come, God sent His son as redeemer and savior. In His son and through Him, He invites men to become, in the Holy Spirit, His adopted children and thus heirs of His blessed life.[41]

Jesus Christ uses every means available to remain relevant to His audience: the example of a precious treasure is astonishing; so also, a fisherman who caught all kinds of sea animals but had to select the good ones while the bad ones are thrown away into eternal damnation. The potential owner of the pearls in the gospel of today will do everything possible to possess them. This explains how Jesus Christ inconveniences Himself to save the dignity of human life as the most precious value in the world. At this challenging time, we ought to pray always, never to lose hope,[42] and to volunteer into discipleship in order to welcome ourselves into the presence of our Lord Jesus Christ and His salvation.

7.5. Seed of Faith

I was born in a farmhouse/community where every healthy person is expected to participate actively in the tilling of the soil for crops to ensure food, cash, and sufficient storage for the season. It is always exciting to experience the first rainfall of the season; farmers prepare their seedlings, selected from the best (corn, maize, millet, sorghum, soya and rice) to be planted either right away or after the second rainfall pending on the level of the rain. It is important to have seedlings that are qualitative, unadulterated, and good enough for planting. The farmer goes to farm to assiduously bury the seedlings, which begin to germinate from three to five days. Due to challenges like bad seedlings, birds pecking, and shortage of rainfall

---

[41] Catechism of the Catholic Church, 9
[42] Luke 18:1

the offshoot of the plants may be adversely affected. Therefore, to boost the outcome, the farmer must replant those areas that are not looking good. The farmer has a lot to contend with: wild animals' havoc, weeds, seasonal drought, and sometimes theft at the time of harvest. The need to take care of the farm constantly cannot be over-emphasized; cultivation and application of chemicals are timely. For the farmer, what he harvests at the end of the year is determined by the level of rainfall, fertility of the soil, and his commitment.

The soil represents the types of members in the Church who hear the gospel and respond to it in faith differently. The faith input determines the outcome of the yield an individual can bear to the glory of God. The seed is the Word, Jesus Christ, the tree of life that gives Himself to friends and loved ones in order to nourish, strengthen, and empower the faithful to be guided, inspired, and be saved from the troubles of this world. Jesus Christ as the seed (Word) in our souls, can ensure a rich harvest of the mercy of God in our life.

The seed(s) that falls by the path has all it takes to be productive, but, for lack of understanding, the devil comes to steal away what is preached. The seed sown on rocky ground exemplifies the gospel that is welcomed with excitement, but due to lack of fundamental basis at any time of trial, such devotee falls apart. The seed among thorns demonstrates how Catholics have all it takes to explore and succeed in their faith encounter but obstructed by a desire to dominate the world and filled with anxiety, we become enslaved by the desire to be powerful, rich, and famous. I tend to resonate with this shackle instead of growing a relationship with my Creator (God) and savior (Jesus Christ) to save myself and help others to do the same. The seed on the rich soil is likened to a Catholic who is ready and willing to share the good, the bad, and the ugly of the faith, which we inherited from our Lord, Jesus Christ. We are expected to become willing disciples. In our faith journey, we need each other for inspiration, guidance, encouragement, and a deeper understanding of God's revelation.

CHAPTER EIGHT:
NAVIGATING THE PATH OF GOD

8.1. I Can See

God can use anything to glorify His name, from the majestic royalty to the lowest peasant. The disciples of Jesus were quick in asking out of curiosity whose sin made the man to be born blind, his sin or his parents'. To which Jesus responded that certain things happen to glorify the name of God. Therefore, as faithful we need to put ourselves in a strategic place where we are guided and protected by faith, grace and the mercy of God in order to be transformed into everlasting children of God forever.[43]

The ministry of Jesus placed all round attention on the needy, especially those that were relegated by the culture, religious practices and everyday interaction. It was likely the blind man did not have the opportunity to participate in the affairs of his community because he was labeled a sinner for being blind. Jesus goes for the soul that obviously needs compassion, care, encouragement and attention; every dignified and legitimate member of the community deserves this. This can be seen when Jesus encountered Zacchaeus, the woman caught in adultery, the ten lepers, and the sick man lowered by his friends.

The healing of the man born blind was not just intended for the man to regain his sight, but to equally use the event to reach out to those who condemn others in ignorance and to have the man participate in discipleship. Since birth he had not seen light, differentiated colors, or traveled to places to acquaint himself, but as soon as he regained his sight, he voluntarily offered himself to be a disciple. The man was able to see not only with his ordinary eyes, but with his spiritual

---

[43] The Book of Jesus, Calvin Miller, p.353

eyes and he could feel some practices were against humanity, which he confronted courageously.

Jesus engaged the religious leaders that are supposed to guide the community, but their inconsiderate treatment was worse than physical blindness; yet they were proud to associate themselves with Moses as a great ancestor. However, as leaders we must be willing to be a light to others; as our vision, understanding, and perception of things may not be the same. That is why we are not made from a place but belong to a particular community to be the inspiration, guidance, and help that is needed to make the best out of life.

One thing that we may need dearly is the courage to bear witness despite challenges and the threats of the opposition. The parents of the man born blind shifted their responsibility as parents (denial mode) for fear of the religious leaders. Were they excited to have their son's sight restored? Yes, but they were not prepared to go through it with the young man to ensure he had the required support and the status he deserved. Our generation thirsts for disciples who would make themselves available to become a voice for those who are voiceless and to always champion justice, equity, tranquility, and the love of God.

8.2. Follow Me

In social media, 'to follow' a person leaves one with whatever the administrator of the account promotes or desires to share, be it Twitter, Facebook, Instagram, or WhatsApp. Some of the followers may get lost due to incompatibility, as the administrator may share only what makes sense to him or her. The various information through the media could be classified as: entertaining, educating, news, explorational, adventurous, dietary, cultural, religious, or political.

In those days, for a Rabbi (master) to command the respect of his disciples, he must know the law, the prophets, and the cultural traditions of his people. It suffices to say, a leader should have a working knowledge of things in his immediate society in order to keep in touch with reality. Jesus politely invited strangers to follow

Him, their compliance has proven the fact that His appearance and conduct was uniquely inviting. Later, in the ministry of Jesus, the confidence of his disciples kept growing up. However, it is not without challenges as Peter noted: "Look, we have left everything and followed you!"[44] Sometimes disciples can feel empty, discouraged, lost in the middle of nowhere or feel irrelevant in one crisis or another.

Arthur Owen Blessit was born in Greenville, Mississippi, USA; and he became a Christian at the age of seven (7). Arthur became a pastor in 1968 in California where he nursed the idea of carrying a gigantic cross to demonstrate his faith. Therefore, on December 25, 1969 he started walking with his passionate cross from Los Angeles to Washington, D.C. However, Arthur took the act of carrying a cross as his vocation, and as such traveled to numerous countries across the globe. By July of 2019, Arthur claims that he has set foot in hundreds of countries and has covered 43,000 miles. In 2015, Guinness World Records awarded him the longest crosswalk pilgrim. The call to follow Jesus is not reserved to a particular person but to all people by choosing positions relevant to the gospel, which at the same time reflect the image and likeness of God.

To be a willing disciple may entail reviewing one's comfort zones in order to turn them into steppingstones not stumbling blocks for the service of God and His ministry. Discipleship is challenging, but notwithstanding, it is more fulfilling and very rewarding; because the volunteer gets more than he/she gives. The disciple develops a bond with those appreciating the message (gospel) through sharing their pains, love, and desires to be better. Eventually, such connection leads to a heart that is willing to share and the avenues that can highlight the potentials that will lead to relating with God and His people deeply. The opening words of Jesus' ministry are: "Repent, for the kingdom of heaven is at hand."[45] As soon as Jesus declared the floor open for a mission, He immediately started recruiting disciples. Recently, the Church had a good number of memberships,

---

[44] Mark 10:28
[45] Matthew 4:17

but not many are willing to volunteer into discipleship. In the words of Jesus, the harvest is rich, but the laborers are few.

8.3. Good-news Response

Saul was a dynamic young man who zealously stood to preserve Jewish traditions across cities, towns, and villages. The disciples of the new religion (Christianity) appeared as a threat to Judaism. Saul volunteered himself to arrest, imprison or kill(eliminate) miscreants. The followers of Christ were chased out of Jerusalem by hostile Jews, like Saul, and the authorities of that time. Saul soon earned a reputation in the destruction of the fragile Christian communities in his surroundings. Then, Saul was dispatched to Damascus, Syria to continue his rage and destruction there. On his way, Saul was struck by the light of the gospel, which led to his conversion. Saul was baptized with the name Paul and henceforth turned his vigor and dynamism into witnessing the gospel to both the Jewish and the Gentiles. Paul is the most traveled apostle, the most prolific writer among the apostles and the evangelists, and the most persecuted and fearless in facing opposition and authorities on matters of faith.

In the Catholic Catechism we read that we are made by God to know Him, love Him, serve Him, and be happy with Him in the next life. By virtue of being created, naturally, we should be drawn towards our Creator, but because of original sin: "I cannot understand my own behavior. I fail to carry out the things I want to do, and I find myself doing the very things I hate... And so, the thing behaving in that way is not myself but sin living in me."[46] We are expected to know God through His revelations, His nature, and the physical structure of the Church. Love is imbedded in our human nature, for instance, a baby does not need the training to respond to the expression of affection from his or her mother. In the same way, in the tone of Saint Augustine, we are made for the sake of God, and our hearts are restless until they rest in you.

In the parable of the two brothers, they were both sent to work in the field; the first one agreed to go, but did not, while the second

---

[46] Matthew 4:17

brother chose not to go, but later went to follow his father's will. Our Catholic faith beckons on all members to accept the challenge of going into the field of evangelism; to serve as consecrated, ordained ministers or lay disciples, those that are longing to hear the gospel. Jesus Christ says that the harvest is rich, but the laborers are few; therefore, we should volunteer to witness, either in person or in kind to parts of the world the gospel is unheard. Yet another challenge that is confronting the Church is the drastic drop of the number of ordained ministers, all ships will require captains to sail. Catechesis should focus on forming intentional disciples that will treat every family as a domestic Church. The evangelization foot soldiers may face multifaceted difficulties due to the economy, policies, inter-religious conflicts, poverty, and cultural and language barriers. The new generation Catholics are conscious of the fact that the Pope, Cardinals, Bishops, priests and nuns cannot finish the work of evangelizing the world. Therefore, every member should participate actively in taking the gospel to every nook and cranny of the world.

8.4. Persecuting the Prophets

The three priests enlisted below served the Church at different times and locations, but they had certain things in common: they were peace loving, trusted God for protection, opted to serve God against human tyranny, killed celebrating Mass, offered their blood as a libation for their sins and the sins of the world. Therefore, Fr. Leo Heinrichs 1908, Denver, Colorado, Saint Archbishop Oscar Romero 1980, El Salvador, Fr. Jacques Hamel 2016, Normandy, France witnessed the gospel under the tutelage of the Catholic Church by their deaths. The sight of nuclear weapons, sophisticated guns, armored cars, jet fighters, scout missiles, and war ships are disturbing. But these victims of the truth relied on the power of the Holy Eucharist for protection. Their blood forever serves as a symbol of sacrifice and dedication to God and His people.

The grace of baptism makes every Catholic a universal priest, a prophet, and a king. By that, it means all members are called into discipleship to bear witness during threats and challenging situations. Dying to self is, embracing the teaching and style of Jesus' life, to be selfless and to put everything at our disposal to serve humanity and give glory to God. Although persecutions started from the inception of the Church, the last 50 years has recorded burned churches, mission schools, rectories, offices, maiming of Christians, killings, destruction of properties, victimization, marginalization, and injustice more than ever before. Jesus Christ relates to what is happening: "I am sending you out like sheep among wolves; so be cunning as serpents and yet as harmless as the doves…You will be hated by all men on account of my name; Whoever stands firm to the end will be saved."[47]

The love of God is mysterious, as He keeps sending messengers to all generations in order to reconstruct the bridge (cross) that is broken by sin. It is as if humanity is losing patience listening to God on how to relate with one another. Whenever Christians are killed for their faith, it is obvious that the perpetrators feel offended by the presence of the truth, the way, and the life: Jesus Christ. "…In the last days there are going to be so difficult times. People will be self-centered and grasping; boastful, arrogant, and rude; disobedient to their parents, ungrateful, irreligious; heartless and unappeasable, preferring their own pleasure to God. They will keep up the outward appearance of religion but will have rejected the inner power of it."[48] The Bible is a love story like no other; God creates things perfectly, but the failure of humanity dearly needs help since he is incapable of helping himself. Therefore, in the Old Testament God reaches out to generations to encourage, guide, and protect them toward salvation. The arrival of Jesus Christ in the New Testament is to complete the process God started in the Old Testament, by fixing humanity where it belongs as its destiny.

---

[47] Matthew 10:16,22

[48] 2Timothy 3:1-5

CHAPTER NINE:
TRANSCENDENTAL ENCOUNTER

9.1. Glorious Journey to Heaven

He was lifted while they looked on, and a cloud took him from their sight.[49] In this age of flying cars, aircraft, jet suits, and rockets it highlights the possibility of a person with a divine power to fly into heaven. Jesus Christ came into the world to bear witness to the peace of God in humility. In His ministry through love, obedience, and service He made reconciliation between God and His people possible. After accomplishing the plans of God in the world (human redemption), He ascended to heaven, in glory, forty days after His resurrection.

In the Old Testament, the prophet Elijah was taken to heaven "Talking as they went, a chariot of fire appeared and horses of fire, coming between the two of them; and Elijah went up to heaven in the whirlwind."[50] In this incident, fifty men were sent to search for Elijah if he could be found on a mountain, a valley, or by a river. However, after three days of searching for Elijah, the messengers came back without any substantial information on where Elijah was and confirmed he had been taken body and soul into heaven. The ascension of Jesus, as well, took place in the presence of His apostles, who advanced His ministry after Him as Elijah prepared Elisha to succeed him.

Jesus having established a spiritual legacy, left His disciples to bear witness based on their faith commitment that radiates love and service. The divine task given to the first set of disciples came with many challenges, as most of them had to face persecution to the point of martyrdom in the process of teaching the gospel. Although

---

[49] Acts of the Apostles 1:9
[50] 2Kings 11-12

they missed the company of their master (Jesus), they immediately started healing the sick, raising the dead, and casting out demons. Despite persecution and stigma, the disciples of Jesus did not give up preaching the gospel. Therefore, conversions were recorded in the thousands and a formulary and rituals (Didache) began to take shape among the early Christians. The first set of Christians witnessed a unique power peculiar to Jesus Christ alone. They witnessed it with conviction and buttressed their claims with practical experiences as eyewitnesses.

At the nick of time, Jesus ascended to enable humanity to put into practice what he taught. To connect the Old Testament events (love of God) to that of the New Testament redemptive role of Jesus Christ, He is portrayed as a bridge (mediator) between God and His people. Due to sin of disobedience, mankind was unable to reconcile a bad relationship with God. Therefore, Jesus Christ asks us to listen and obey the instructions of God as the Blessed Virgin Mary, the saints, angels, holy men and women do. Perfection may not be reached in this world; Jesus Christ ascends to complete our incompleteness and to intercede on our behalf to restore our lost glory. We should be conscious of one fact, that we are loved by God unconditionally in Jesus Christ.

The Old Testament messiah finally arrived in the first century in the person of Jesus Christ. The savior of the world lived for thirty years before starting His three years of ministry. His sermons laid emphasis on the love and mercy of God, which He further displayed in his care for the needy. Even those against his mission testified to the fact that He did things uniquely and with authority. He was able to overcome human weakness, disobedience, and pride; His triumph, therefore, brought glory to humanity forever. Before His ascension into heaven, Jesus mentored His disciples to carry on His ministry to the ends of the world. The impeccable character He inculcated into the life of the disciples enabled them to conquer their challenges and difficulties through unconditional love. The first set of Christians faced persecution to the extent of running into catacombs, a place where the dead members of their community were buried. The early Christians had to endure challenges, even if it meant dying for the sake of the gospel. However, the continuity of the gospel was at stake as the key leaders were killed in numbers. Therefore, they had to preserve the Didache (teachings) handed over to them by the Lord for future generations. The parting words of Jesus Christ were, "Go, therefore, make disciples of all the nations; baptize them in the name of the Father and of the Son and of the Holy Spirit, ...and know that I am with you always; yes, to the end of time."[51] The great commissioning by our Lord, Jesus Christ serves as an open invitation for every Catholic to willingly embrace the responsibility of serving the gospel either by the use of words, actions, or resources. The tone of Jesus Christ portrays a sense of urgency, which means in whatever situation a Christian finds himself or herself in, the responsibility to evangelize should be given due attention. The coming of Jesus into the world and His ministerial style provoked the authorities of His days, who sought for His elimination. However, He came to complete the law and the prophets; therefore, He restored human salvation through obedience, humility, and selfless service to God and His people. The passion, crucifixion, and death of Jesus Christ point to a sacrificial lamb that chose to do the will of God rather than disobey. The departure of the physical Jesus from the face of the earth leaves us with the assignment of putting into practice what we have received through His teaching and action. Although Jesus Christ has gone to the Father, His Church (Catholic) keeps His hope alive. Every Christian is expected to live by the virtues that will configure one into another Christ from one generation to the next. There are fascinating stories of the dynamics of politics, economic strategists, cultural dominance, and educational excellence, but the greatest story ever told in our human setting is the salvation of humanity through Jesus Christ.

9.2. Bear the Gospel

The disciples of Jesus are required to exercise some discipline and ascetic style of life. Those with the noble privilege of bearing witness to the gospel should realize that it is all-encompassing, as everything should be in perspective to send the divine message

---

[51] Matthew 28:19-20

home. Jesus is clamoring for self-control, detachment, and a sense of purpose in pursuing the course of the gospel. However, His disciples realized the difficulties and challenges of carrying out His mission and ministry in a society that has attention to different values. They keenly listened to the instructions of Jesus and followed them closely; therefore, they achieved a lot to the glory of God.

What is the latest update on the discipline of discipleship? Distractions may come by way of electronics, video games, mobility, socialization, jets, mansions, fashions, sports, secular music, and extra finances. To a disciple, Jesus should serve as the center of his or her mission, otherwise, bearing witness may be in a crisis as an essential ingredient for service is severed from the body of the Church. The in-thing in the world is the drive to accumulate wealth with a desire to dominate the world. If being wealthy ensures a peaceful state, the wealthiest people in the world should have been the happiest and the most fulfilled. Human salvation through Jesus Christ is the greatest thing to have ever happened to humanity; therefore, all things should be made steppingstones to God and His salvation. The multiplication of religions and denominations is ongoing; however, it is disheartening as the original mission and ministry of Jesus Christ loses its bearing. The celebration of human shortcomings and an emphasis on what a disciple can do in order to mesmerize His faithful undermines the enormity of the message. The classification of witnesses may be categorized according to order of priorities: some preachers lay emphasis on making money for God while others may want to hypnotize their followers through healing and deliverance sessions. In any case, Jesus clearly wants His gospel to be kept unadulterated and undiluted through all generations. The modern world has witnessed great moments when the gospel of Jesus Christ has taken root in places that are completely isolated, dry, and obsolete. The apparitions of Jesus and His Mother in different parts of the world, from one generation to another have highlighted the light of the gospel that has been there since the first century. Jesus Christ obviously is the Word, and His Holy Spirit is the interpreter to every generation; as such, volunteers should cooperate with the will of God by keeping His instructions on how to bear witness. It is ridiculous how preachers approach converts with tons of material wealth, with security escorts, feeling better than the recipients of the gospel, and emphasis is laid on an individual financial contribution to the progress of the gospel. The first commandment of the Decalogue requires the faithful to have no attachment to anything but to God alone. Therefore, Jesus Christ is not only calling on His followers to set themselves apart for God alone but to likewise teach others to do the same.

9.3. An Illumined Church

The founder and leader of the first Christian community of believers, Jesus Christ died horribly, it devastated His disciples. Out of fear they locked their doors and could not move freely in public. After His resurrection, Jesus appeared to His disciples several times to raise their confidence. In His teachings, Jesus emphasized bearing witness to the gospel, especially in those areas yet to listen to the good news. As the disciples were sent to teach and preach the gospel, the gift of the Holy Spirit guided and empowered them to serve the gospel, in season and out of season. The execution of Jesus Christ affected His disciples to the point of scandalizing their understanding and disorganizing their faithful commitment to their master. Moreover, the future of His mission and His ministry appeared uncertain and shattered by the way His life ended. The arrival of the Holy Spirit on the disciples, on Pentecost day ignited a quenched fire or a sort of turn over (metanoia); the disciples instantly became fearless, courageous, and voluntarily faced their challenges of bearing witness to the gospel. They appeared dynamic and had the relevant language to relate His message of gladness to the world. The motivation to build the Tower of Babel was marred by mischief; therefore, the workers encountered misunderstandings, conflicts, and disharmony, and as a result such discrepancies led to the abandonment of the project. The Church appreciates the use of signs and symbols; therefore, it portrays the presence of the Holy Spirit in the form of a flame of fire or dove. This is to demonstrate the dynamism and the innocence of the Holy Spirit in guiding the disciples of Jesus into salvation. One may ask, without the gift of the Holy Spirit, what would have become of the Church? It would have made its mission more difficult or even impossible. In any case, God is envisioned in the flames of fire; "There the angel of Yahweh appeared to him (Moses) in the shape of a flame of fire, coming from the middle of a bush."[52] "Yahweh went before them, by day in the form of a pillar of cloud to show them the way, and by night in the form of a pillar of fire to give them light: thus they could continue their march by day and by night."[53] The use of paschal candles, candles during Mass (altar), and tabernacle lights highlight the presence of the Holy (God) of Holies (Saints and angels), which beckons on the faithful to pay homage to Him, just like Moses did in the burning bush. Similarly, the light of the star led the three wise men to pay homage to baby Jesus. In Genesis's narrative account, darkness, chaos, and disorder covered the world; but God saw the need to create light and order. The gifts of the Holy Spirit are wisdom, understanding, piety, knowledge, counsel, God's fear, and fortitude. They are enough to keep us in a complete relationship with God forever.

9.4. A Blazing Fire

Jesus' proclamation of the kingdom is a refining and purifying fire. His message that meets with acceptance or rejection will be a source of conflict and dissension even within families.[54] The arrival of Jesus ushered in a new perspective into looking at life generally. As a spiritual revolutionary, He figuratively looked at His message of love, hope, truth, and peace as fire that should be burning in all relationships with God and His people.

In the Old Testament, fire played a pivotal role in representing the presence of God, especially during sacrifices. Therefore, the patriarchs, the priests, and the prophets encountered God at different events and places through the means of fire. Xavier Leon-Dufour notes that; "Fire in the Old Testament traditions has value only as a sign, which must transcend to find God."[55]

---

[52] Exodus 3:20
[53] Exodus 13:21
[54] Fireside Catholic Youth Bible P.1116
[55] Dictionary of Biblical Theology p.180

The Pentecost experience recorded in the New Testament presents us disciples that were timid, confused, and scared to even walk outside the doors of their safe environment. But the arrival of the Holy Spirit in the form of flames of fire turned everything around. They instantly became fearless, courageous, and resolute witnesses of the gospel. "Do not put out the Spirit's."[56] Do not quench it! Let the baptism with the Holy Spirit and fire cleanse you and empower you. Do not resist, "let it burn."

Conflicts and divisions may arise within family settings as a result of differences in opinions and understanding. To some members of the family, they may choose to be with Jesus as their way, the truth, and their source of life, while the rest of the family members may doubt the existence of God and Jesus Christ as a savior. This may bring about tension in the family, tension between denominations, and tension among different faiths.

The Bishop of the Diocese of Zaria, George J. Dodo located in Northern Nigeria, was celebrating 8:00AM Mass at Christ the King Cathedral on June 17, 2012, when multiple explosives erupted which killed ten people. It was a scary experience; the thunderous sound, the destruction of the building, and the shock of such an encounter left the victims with a long time of trauma. But the following Sunday the Church was filled, as members preferred to die in the Church than to die elsewhere. There is always a burning sensation in our relationship with Jesus. We must be willing disciples through witnessing.

---

[56] 1 Thessalonians 5:197

CHAPTER TEN:
DIVINE REPARATION

10.1. The Power of Forgiveness

The 1994 Rwandan genocide left the citizens of the country with many lessons. Rwanda is a country located in East Africa, with a population of 12.3 million as of 2018. A survey after the war reported that about 800,000 died during the war. However, the government that succeeded, led by Paul Kagame, wanted the citizens to reconcile their differences. Therefore, reconciliatory commissions were set up across the country. These commissions aimed at bringing the perpetrators of killings and their victims together for healing and posterity. Ann-Marie Uwimana, one of the traumatized, lost her husband and four children. Eventually, Celestin, one of the perpetrators of the dastardly act, got his way back to the same community with Ann-Marie. Virtually, the world of Ann- Marie was shattered; but her parish priest gave her the need to forgive her offenders in order to heal herself completely. "Unable to forgive is like cancer, it eats you from the inside," noted by a mother whose sixteen years old son was shot by a trigger crazy man. Ann-Marie forgave Celestin and started a friendship of sharing meals, faith and other challenges. The dynamics of forgiveness are transformative which leads to eternal peace.

The God in the Old Testament is a forgiving Creator, and a Father: His encounter with Adam and Eve leaves us with a Father who tolerated their disobedience. And He further opened new opportunities for humanity, in order not to be condemned by original sin. This is the reason why God sends priests, kings, and prophets to reconcile the gap between Him and His chosen ones. "Look, I am going to send my messenger to prepare a way before me. And the lord you are seeking will suddenly enter his Temple; and the angel of the covenant whom you are longing for, yes, he is coming, says Yahweh Sabaoth."[57]

In the New Testament, Jesus Christ fulfills the law and the prophets as the Old Testament foretold. It is about the love of God and His unmerited mercy upon humanity in this troublesome world. Therefore, Jesus Christ is the bridge to our Father, Creator. His cross is a symbol of triumph and glory. To benefit from His suffering and sacrifice, we must come to Him as the way, the truth, and the life. Jesus Christ in His messages to Saint Sister Faustina Kowalska says, "When you go to confession, to this fountain of my mercy, the Blood and Water which came forth from my Heart always flows down upon your soul and ennobles it. Every time you go to confession, immerse yourself in my mercy, with great trust, so that I may pour the bounty of my grace upon your soul. When you approach the confessional, know this, I myself am waiting there for you. I am only hidden by the priest, but I myself act in your soul. Here the misery of the soul meets the God of mercy. Tell souls that from this fount of mercy, souls draw graces solely with the vessel of trust. If their trust is great, there is no limit to my generosity. The torrents of grace inundate humble souls. The proud always remain in poverty and misery, because my grace turns away from them to humble souls."[58]

10.2. To Forgive is Divine

The Indian advocate for non-violent freedom struggles, Mahatma Gandhi in a famous speech, says, "An eye for an eye makes the world blind."[59] Gandhi is of the opinion if every bad act is retaliated, how will the world look? Revenge and destruction frenzy? And will anyone have the guts to criticize or condemn an act when observed to be wrong? Gandhi suggests overcoming evil with goodness, wrong doings with righteousness, hate with love. Only then, the presence of God will make sense, as He encourages us to be our neighbor's

---

[57] Malachi 3:1-2
[58] Divine Mercy in My Soul; Retrieved 08/20/2020.
[59] Shmoop Quotes; Retrieved 08/20/2020.

keeper. Otherwise, the world may degrade into chaotic situations which may lead humanity into conflicts, fights, wars, and tension.

The Jewish cultural background of Jesus and his disciples confronts their sense of judgment either to preserve the tradition or enact a new way of looking at forgiveness. Tradition teaches that it's an eye for an eye, tooth for tooth, which means whoever offends you pays that person in the same measure. Peter put this question to clarify issues; will it be business as usual as stipulated by the Torah, or a review is necessary? Jesus introduces a new concept, "forgiveness," and for those who are desirous of retaliating should meticulously count to 490 times before any revenge takes place. It appeared obvious that Jesus Christ is stressing the fact that forgiveness is for infinity, as we do not deserve forgiveness from God; out of His mercy and magnanimity He forgives our imperfections.

In Hausa, my native language, there is a saying, laifi tudu ne (sin is like a mountain) one climbs his or hers to see the fault of others. People may easily see the sin of others in our society, which may be a way of presuming the position of self-righteousness. Spiritual Theologians are unanimous in noticing how small (venial) sins destroy spiritual lives more than capital (mortal) sins. The small sins are like sand, they deter us from moving in our spiritual journey; on the other hand, mortal sins, because of their enormity and their impact, they become steppingstones back to God, a merciful and receptive Father. "Jesus said to them, 'I tell you solemnly, tax collectors and prostitutes are making their way into the kingdom of God before you.'"[60]

The generous mercy of God is unprecedented, as we have seen in the Biblical account; it is divine love initiated by God that leads us to the suffering, death, and resurrection of Jesus. Therefore, the cross of Jesus is a symbol of forgiveness, hope, salvation, reconciliation, and restoration. God displeased Himself, away from His comfort zone to the point of humiliating His only beloved son, to secure human redemption. What should register in our minds is that humans are interrelated through all generations in relation to God. Therefore,

---

[60] Matthew 21:31

we must work frantically to live, promote, and teach righteousness; to pass the culture to next generations.

10.3 Casting and Binding Demons

Louis Melgoza, 58, who primarily does estate and business consulting developed an interest in studying demons (demonology). Melgoza is not just having a theological study on demonology, but he has heard, seen, felt, and fought them several times. He is among the privileged few lay persons and priests that are certified by Rome to perform spiritual exercises to free those troubled by evil spirits. Melgoza gives talks and hints on how to identify evil attacks, and how to protect oneself. Although, he assisted priests several times to perform exorcisms reserved to ordained ministers (Catholic Priests) alone. Louis will always want his audience to know that there may not be an explanation for the natural cause of our calamities but sometimes there may be supernatural ones. The ongoing spiritual warfare is sometimes seen as part of life, but there is more to that. The bizarre stories of ghost apparitions are all over; we must take into account that many priests and kind-hearted people have been killed by evil spirits to destabilize Godly settings. Most exorcists opine that the demons cannot have access into you without one's consent. There is a need to be smart and alert.[61]

On a faithful day, my administrative assistant received a distress call from a family whose house was ravaged by the ghost of a lady that passed during a short visit. It is important to note that some houses and humans may be troubled by evil spirits. To pray with the family at the scene of the passage, I picked up my prayer book, stole, and holy water and headed to the house in question. As soon as I arrived, I noticed the restlessness of the family, who went ahead to show me where it all happened. We started prayers right away and the ghost attempted to go into the woman of the house, but prayer persistence made the ghost go away through the kitchen window blind. The presence of ghosts is real, but they cannot cause any harm to humans without the use of a physical body.

---

[61] Casting out demons: Melgoza assists in exorcism, The Kentucky Started, Randy Patrick, Retrieved 01/11/2021.

The second story is about a man that belongs to a cult (masonry) that made him have several vehicle accidents in his life, frustrated for violating their covenant. He visited the parish office to request deliverance, but I asked him if he would be patient to wait through the long prayers. The gentleman patiently waited for the end of the prayers; and after a few weeks, he came to the office to say things got better as a result of the prayers. Normal prayers of exorcism may take hours depending on the type of evil spirit and level of commitment of the victim. In the gospel, Jesus Christ assumed a position of leadership over his disciples and uniquely controls the demons that trouble the chosen people set apart for God. The audience listening to Jesus notices something different compared to other teachers because He taught with authority and conviction.

10.4. Get Well Soon

The sacraments of reconciliation and anointing of the sick heal the soul and the body of the patient. In my ministerial life as a priest, I served the sick members at homes, hospitals, retirement homes, and clinics. What stands out clearly is that the patients appear calm and submissive to the will of God. There is a need to pray with the patients treating temporal, terminal illnesses and the ones actively dying. Some of the patients may be bedridden for several years and therefore may be unable to attend Church sacraments regularly. For the sick and the home bound, whenever spiritual instruments such as communion, holy water, crucifix, and holy oil are brought, they feel excited to partake. There is a sense of urgency in the ministry of Jesus Christ to cover space and time, in order to redeem a situation corrupted by sin (disobedience). The opportunity we get through Jesus Christ is to establish a relationship with a God whose grace, love, mercy, and generosity we squander. As we feed the hungry, clothe the naked, heal the sick, and help the needy, we are in our own way putting the teachings of Jesus Christ into action. The essence of the miracles in the gospels were to re-integrate the beneficiaries into the community, not to draw attention to Jesus. As such, some of the beneficiaries received instruction to observe secrecy. Jesus did miracles to fulfill the law and the prophets. In Genesis, we meet a God who perfected His creation and entrusted its care to humanity.

It is human to be sick, and on the other hand it is by the grace of God that we are healed. The question that may be asked is, why should righteous people suffer sicknesses or misfortunes? The experience of Job in the Old Testament drives the message home,[62] the ordeal of an obedient servant of God. Job was prosperous, powerful, and famous. But the devil thought he was faithful to God because of his exploit. As such, the devil asked to test his faithfulness by destroying his family, his riches, his friends, and his health. However, Job endured to the end which attracted reparations (multiplication of what he lost) from God. As gold is tested by fire so also the righteous of God may be tested through temptations. Triduum (paschal mystery) highlights a Jesus that appeared vibrant, dynamic, healthy, and full of life, who willingly embraced horrible torture that made him completely sick/weak. The Roman Catholic Church anoints the five places of Jesus' wounds when anointing a patient (the forehead, the chest, the palms, and the feet). This is to configure the suffering of the patient into the suffering of Jesus Christ. Jesus Christ out of volition, embraced His sickness and humiliating death for the sake of human redemption. The disciples of Jesus were curious to know whose sin made the young man to be born blind. The response of Jesus Christ was it happened to glorify God. Through centuries humanity treated its ailments with the means a generation could afford. But the days of Jesus Christ were unique because of His power to heal the sick and raise the dead.

10.5. The Stigma of Sin is like that of Leprosy

The inception of COVID-19 was scary, as the symptoms of the virus were uncertain and its mode of operation unknown. This made the residents of Nova Scotia, Canada to stigmatize those suspected to have the virus. The ill-treatment/hostility by family members, relatives, health workers, and the general public made things more difficult for patients. The palpable fear was a result of insufficient information on how the virus is contracted and how one could protect himself/herself. The reality of having the virus may be devastating for lack of regular medication, the isolation, and

---

[62] Job 1:10-12

the depression that may set in as a result of uncertainties. However, COVID-19 has changed the world order as businesses, religious centers, and public activities may not approach life as done before.

A leprosarium located in Ghana, West Africa is situated far away from the community so as to isolate the lepers. A nursing mother with a skin (leprous) infection can be seen cut off from her daily routines: interaction, food variety, freedom, and caring for her dependents. The stigma may be so devastating and depressing as patients are confined to their colony. A child born in such an environment has to struggle to survive a bizarre style of life and may likely be infected by the disease. Obviously, children like that may become a liability throughout their existence, unable to cater for themselves and for their loved ones. Finally, their only means of survival will be to beg in the streets. The loss of their fingers does not take away the image and likeness of God (dignity) from them.

In the days of Jesus Christ on earth, lepers were classified as sinners, and unclean, and therefore the general public were instructed to relate with them carefully. To alert the public of their presence, a bell was tied round their necks and with a loud voice the lepers would keep repeating the word "unclean." This was to alert the members of society to not have any form of contact with them. In the gospel of today, the leper courageously approached Jesus to tender his request, "If you want to, you can make me clean." Jesus Christ in His usual attitude of saving a bad situation and turning it into a better one, went further to touch an unclean man. As soon as his fingers were restored, Jesus instructed him to go to a priest for verification and re-integration into society. But, the excitement of such an encounter led the healed leper to become a disciple, witnessing the greatness of God. The God of miracles is still with us; therefore, approach Him like the leper in total submission to His will. We can learn lessons from this encounter in whatever situation we may find ourselves. Jesus can do something right away; we should believe and trust Him. Furthermore, we should not wait for Jesus to look for us. Instead, we should go to Him as a friend and as our savior.

CONCLUSION

An important question that may come to the mind of the reader may be, how can a disciple participate in discipleship effectively. It always gives the opportunity to draw others to Christ, not by the use of words alone but through the application of gospel values in every given situation.

Our life approach should be deeply immersed in the scripture to get lessons from biblical models and from their wealth of experience, especially at those moments where they encountered God while carrying out the assignments given to them.

Prayer keeps God and His people in touch with the disciple; it provides nourishment to a Christian soul to support and strengthen a spiritual journey that may be confronted by challenges and difficulties. Furthermore, it is a means by which a disciple is given the opportunity to grow in faith through a partnership with God.

The life of a disciple should be enriched by the values of the gospel; as such, when going through everyday challenges, there should be complete submission to the will of God in the light of the gospel.

The aim of every Christian disciple should be to raise a community with God as the center and all other references point to Him, especially in a chaotic situation. Such communities should be guided and be sustained through sharing the basic things of life: food, drink, clothes, accommodation, visitation to the sick, burying the dead, and visitation to those in prison.

BIBLIOGRAPHY

1. Albl, C. Martin. *The Church: Christ in the World Today.*

2. Catechism of the Catholic Church, vol. 9.

3. Dufour, Leon. *Dictionary of Biblical Theology.* The Word Among Us. Press, 2000.

4. Liguori, Alphonsus. *The Twelve Steps to Holiness and Salvation.*

5. McKenzie, John, S.J. *Dictionary of the Bible.* A Touchstone Book, 1995.

6. Miller, Calvin. *The Book of Jesus.*

7. Morrow, Louis. *Fireside Catholic Youth Bible.*

8. *The Bathroom LOL Book*

9. La Ravoire. *My Catholic Faith*

10. Weddell, Sherry A. *Forming Intentional Disciples: The Path to Knowing and Following Jesus.* Our Sunday Visitor.

11. *The Jerusalem Bible.* Edited by Alexander Jones, Doubleday, 1966